A Guide to

THE ORCHIDS OF SIKKIM

A Guide to

THE ORCHIDS OF SIKKIM

Being a Guide to the Identification of those species of Orchids found between the terai and the northern frontier of independent Sikkim including the Chumbi Valley and British Bhutan

By

PAUL BRUHL, D.Sc.,

Professor of Botany, University of Calcutta

GYAN

Published by

GYAN

Gyan Publishing House
5, Ansari Road
Daryaganj, New Delhi-110002
Phone: 011-47034999, 9811692060
E-mail: books@gyanbooks.com

Distribution Network
gyanbooks.com
India, USA, Canada, UK, Australia, France

ISBN : 978-81-212-1376-9 (HB)
First Published, 1926

2nd Impression 2021

Printed at: Gyan Press, Delhi.

A Guide to THE ORCHIDS OF SIKKIM
Author: PAUL BRUHL

Dedicated to the Memory of

SIR GEORGE KING AND MR. ROBERT PANTLING

and to all lovers of Orchids

FOREWORD.

It was during a nine months' stay in the Sikkim-Himalayas in the years 1907 and 1908 that I practically completed a "Guide to the Flora of Sikkim and the Chumbi Valley" on a plan similar to that adopted in the present "Guide to the Orchids of Sikkim." Official duties into which botanical studies did not enter prevented my putting the finishing touch to the work, and when in 1912 I retired from Government Service and left Calcutta for Bangalore, I left the bulky manuscript in what I thought was safe custody. A return to a more congenial intellectual atmosphere in 1918 prompted me to take up the work again, but to my utter dismay I discovered that the manuscript could not be traced. I resolved then to make a new start and to make a beginning with what is one of the chief glories of the rich flora of Sikkim—the Orchids. The present "Guide" is the result of my labours. These labours have been greatly facilitated by the late Sir George King's and Robert Pantling's monumental work on "The Orchids of the Sikkim-Himalaya," published as volume VIII in the Annals of the Royal Botanic Garden, Calcutta. The thoroughness with which the two authors did do their work is seen from the fact that since the publication of that volume, which is accompanied by numerous plates, only two undoubtedly new species of Orchids have been discovered in the Sikkim-Himalayas. For localities, altitudes, flowering times and the colours of the flowers I am largely indebted to Sir George King's and Mr. Pantling's work.

The present guide is written for use in field and forest, in green-house and the verandah, where whole living plants are available for examination; people who are under the impression that satisfactory and expeditious identifications can be effected by means of little bits off the top or by fragments of leaves are greatly mistaken. Dried herbarium specimens—mere corpses—are ugly and difficult to analyse, and there is much to be learnt about plant life by its study in field and forest.

The guide is chiefly written for non-botanists, although it may not be without use even to the professed student of botany. Like its more comprehensive forerunner, it has been tested over and over again, and that much to its own advantage, by friends who are interested in plants without pretending to be expert botanists. The terms used are mostly ordinary English terms, and such terms as rhizome, pseudobulb, scape, calyx, corolla, stamens, anthers, pollen, ovary, inflorescence, petiole, peduncle, pedicel, are probably sufficiently well known not to be in need of elaborate explanations. There is nothing particularly "scientific" about Anglo-Latin and Anglo-Greek terms; botanical books written in Germanic and Slavonic languages manage to get along quite well without them. A few terms are explained further on and the accompanying plate will be helpful.

The key to genera and species is worked out strictly on the dichotomous plan, that is to say, it rigorously proceeds by alternatives. Nearly always there are more than one pair of alternatives, so that if one pair leaves some doubt in the mind of the one who uses the guide, the other alternative or alternatives will lay the doubt.

Most of the characters referred to can be made out by the naked eye without dissection. The only dissection that will be useful to make, besides sometimes a cross-section through spur or ovary, is a longitudinal section from the base of the flower upwards and passing along the plane of symmetry, that is, through the middle line of the lip and the odd sepal, thus halving the "column" lengthways. A razor or sharp pen-knife are the only tools required for the purpose. Some species of Oberonia, Microstylis, Habenaria, and a few other genera will necessitate the use of a lens; as the human eye is a valuable possession, I should recommend the use of a Zeiss or Leitz single aplanatic folding lens magnifying ten times, which is sufficient for most identifying work of flowering plants; the double or triple folding lenses sold in the market are of little use and strain the eye.

The following will illustrate the use of the two keys. Let us suppose that we deal with a specimen of Dendrobium chrysanthum, an orchid growing on the branches of trees between the 3,000 and 6,000 feet levels. We refer first to the Key to the Genera.

The plant is epiphytic; we are, therefore, directed to **67**; the sepals are nearly free from each other and not connected into a tube: **69**; the plant bears leaves at flowering time: **71**: the leaves are nearly flat, not at all terete: **77**; the stem is of the ordinary kind and does not form or consist of pseudobulbs: **98**; the lip is not spurred: **115**; the sepals exceed 1 cm. in length: **127**; the column is extended at its base into a " foot ": **128**; the foot is not extended into lobes or horns: **129**; the pollinia are four in number forming a single row: **Dendrobium.**

This takes us to page 54.

We start from **1**. The stems grow close together; the alternative does not fit at all: **2**; the stems are of ordinary shape and much longer than 3 inches: **5**; the leaves are leathery and mostly more than 5 cm. in length: **7**; the flowers together form a conspicuous raceme and not a nodding head, and the stem is neither slender-obovate nor spindle-shaped: **9**; the inflorescence is showy: **20**; the stem is approximately cylindrical, the sepals are ovate-oblong, the petals broadly oblong or elliptic, the flowers yellow and more than 18 mm. across: **23**; the stem is pendulous (hanging down): **25**; the flowering stem bears leaves: **26**; the stem is 80 cm. long or less, the yellow flowers are in clusters of 2—4 on the nodes of the upper part of the stem, the lip has two brownish-purple patches and a felty rim: **Dendrobium chrysanthum.**

The names of persons following the names of genera and species are those of botanists who first introduced the name or combination of names. Of these botanists Roxburgh, Wallich, Griffith, King and Prain have held the appointment of Superintendents of the Sibpur Botanical Gardens; Hooker fil. is Sir Joseph Hooker, who for many years was Director of the Kew Gardens; so was his father, Sir William Jackson Hooker; Sir Joseph Hooker, one of the great authorities on Orchids, travelled in Chota Nagpur, Sikkim and the Khasia Hills and edited that great work, the "Flora of British India." John Lindley (1799–1865) was Professor of Botany at the University of London from 1829–1860 and was one of the greatest authorities on Orchids at his time. So was also Reichenbach fil., the son of the great German systematic botanist Reichenbach, the Director of the Dresden Botanical Garden. Robert Pantling was for many years an official employed in the Mangpu Cinchona Plantation; he was an excellent draughtsman and painter and possessed a most intimate knowledge of the orchids of Sikkim.

Of the genera of Orchids occurring in the Simla region only one—Hemipilia—is not found in Sikkim; Neottia listerioides is the same as Listera Lindleyana of this Guide.

Of the 453 species of Sikkim Orchids about 53 per cent. occur also in the Assam region, especially in the Khasia Hills, and 28 per cent. are found also in Nipal. About 90 species of Orchids met with in the Khasia Hills do not occur in Sikkim and about 16 species of chiefly Western Nipal Orchids have not been recorded from Sikkim and Bhotan.

The species Key of Bulbophyllum has been accidentally displaced; its proper place is immediately after the species Key of Dendrobium on page 67. The displacement will not cause the slightest inconvenience to the user of the "Guide." The reader is requested to take the key to the species of the genera Ione and Sunipia on pages 207 and 208 as replacing the species Key of Ione on pages 101 and 102, which may be considered as cancelled.

P. B.

INDEX OF SPECIES

Species marked † occur between the 500 and 4,000 feet levels, those marked with an asterisk are met with between 4,000 and 8,000 feet, those marked with 0 grow above 8,000 feet; species marked †* will mostly be found at altitudes ranging from 3,000 to 6,000 feet, and those marked *0 between 6,000 and 10,000 feet. Most of the lower level species inhabit the forests bordering the valleys of the Tista and its tributaries.

(1) The name Microstylis callosa is taken from plate 20 of King' and Pantling's monograph; in the text the plant is described under the name of M. Scottii; its proper name is M. calophylla, Reichenbach fil.

KEY TO THE GENERA.

1\. Terrestrial—rooting in the ground, not detachable without digging the plant out, sometimes saprophytic, growing on humus or parasitic on the roots of other plants, rarely growing on the vertical face of sandstone rocks **2**

— Epiphytic—growing on the stems and branches of shrubs and trees, sometimes found on the ground or among moss on the surface of rocks, having in most cases dropped down from trees and then easily detachable from the substratum .. **67**

2\. Parts of the flowers, including the lip, similar in shape and size, the flowers therefore nearly regular; anthers two, quite separate; ovary three-celled.

Apostasia. p. 136.

— Lip distinctly, and usually markedly different in shape from sepals and petals; the flower symmetrical with regard to a plane passing through the middle line of the lip and containing the axis of ovary and column **3**

3\. Lip consisting nearly entirely either of an ovoid bag with an open or nearly closed mouth or having the shape of a short-cylindric vessel with round bottom; edge of the mouth reflexed or crenulate; anthers two; ovary 1- or 3-celled.

Cypripedium. p. 195.

— Lip flat or concave, either entire or lobed, with or without one or two spurs or a pouch-shaped protrusion or only gibbous at its base, rarely only consisting of a stout spur with hardly any end- and side-lobes; another one, ovary one-celled .. 4

4. Growing on the face of sandstone rocks; leaves pendulous, linear-oblong; petals and lip large, white, orbicular-reniform. **Diplomeris. p. 194.**

— Rooting in soil or leaf-mould or parasitic on the roots of other plants 5

5. Without any leaves at any time; stem, floral axis, and bracts pale-coloured, yellowish or brown, very rarely the upper scales of the scape pale-green; parts of the flowers commonly brown or yellow, rarely greenish, white or blackish-purple 6

— Leaves either contemporaneous with the flowers, or leaves and flowers appearing at different times; the flowers either on leafy shoots or on separate leafless shoots .. 16

6. Tubers several, arranged in a chain; pedicels greatly elongating after flowering time; flowers 8—9 mm. in length, forming an irregular raceme. **Didymoplexis. p. 152.**

— Tubers single or absent 7

7. Flowers not exceeding 4 mm. in length or diameter 8

— Flowers at least 10 mm. as measured lengthwise or either from tip to tip of the lateral sepals or from the tip of the dorsal sepal to the tip of the lip **11**

8. Flowers 3—4 mm. across; ovary not twisted, lip therefore superior **9**

— Flowers less than 2 mm. in length or diameter; ovary twisted, lip inferior .. **10**

9. Flowering axis rising from a globular or a stout, somewhat oblique and irregularly oblong tuber emitting only a few root-fibres, sepals linear-oblong, the lateral sepals and the petals recurved or reflexed; lip with two lanceolate-oblong somewhat falcate basal lobes.

Two species of **Microstylis. p. 44.**

— Flowering axis rising from a thin, horizontal rhizome emitting a dense bush of thin rootlets; sepals spreading, linear, recurved near their tips; lip concave, without basal or lateral lobes.

One species of **Aphyllorchis. p. 153.**

10. Stem decumbent at its basal part; flowering axis erect, terminating in a dense, many-flowered, narrow-cylindrical spike; lip elliptical, entire. **Risleya. p. 145.**

— Flowering axis erect, rising from a short and rather thick, nearly horizontal rhizome; flowers 2—3, sub-terminal; lip transversely elliptic (when flattened out) with a basal sub-erect, two-lobed, tongue-like process.

Pantlingia. p. 151.

11. Lip spurred, spur as long as, or shorter than the lip, club-shaped; rhizome stout-conical or coralloid. **Epipogum. p. 147.**

— Spur wanting **12**

12. Sepals united into a cylindrical tube, somewhat swollen at the base and three-toothed at the mouth; stem very slender, 30—40 cm. long, about 2 mm. thick; flowers 3—4, nodding. **Gastrodia. p. 152.**

— Sepals free from each other; stem at least 3 mm. thick near its base .. **13**

13. Flowering plant not exceeding 12 cm. in height; sepals fleshy; lip slipper-shaped, posterior part forming an open bowl, the edges of the anterior part nearly in contact. **Yoania. p. 108.**

— Flowering plant at least 20 cm. in height, erect or climbing; anterior part of lip flat or concave, always open **14**

14. Flowering plant 20—30 cm. high; lip 2—3 times as long as the sepals, two-lobed, narrowing towards the base, margins recurved. One species of **Listera. p. 148.**

— Flowering plant more than 40 cm. long; lip shorter or little longer than the sepals, concave **15**

15. Stem erect, less than 80 cm. in height; inflorescence a simple, rather lax raceme. **Aphyllorchis. p. 153.**

— Stem either erect and 120—150 cm. in height, or extensively climbing; inflorescence a compound raceme or a much-branched panicle. **Galeola. p. 154.**

16. Inflorescence inserted either on a stout, irregularly oblong, more or less horizontal, 7—15 cm. long and 4—7 cm. thick tuber, or on the side of a large spherical undivided or forked tuber measuring up to 8 cm. in diameter, or on a large depressed-globular cake-like tuber covered with nodules **17**

— Inflorescence rising from the top, side, or base of a globular, ovoid, or sub-cylindric tuber or pseudobulb or at the base and side of a false stem formed by the bases of leaves or either lateral or terminal on a leafy stem **18**

17. Tuber not covered with nodules; sepals and petals ovate, elliptic or lanceolate, spreading or connivent, petals relatively broader, lip not more than twice as long as broad; flowers not imbricate. **Eulophia. p. 109.**

— Tuber covered with nodules; sepals and petals oblanceolate, their lower parts nearly parallel; basal portion of the lip nearly linear, its end-lobe with a fleshy appendage at its base, length of lip at least six times the width of the end-lobe; flowers closely imbricate forming a dense, conical spike. **Cremastra. p. 112.**

18. Flower-bearing axis devoid of true leaves, rising directly from a tuber or rootstock or from the apex, side or base of a pseudobulb, or, in some case, from the axil of a scale-like leaf-sheath below the upper leafy part of the stem .. **19**

— Inflorescence from the axil of a true leaf or terminal on a well-developed leafy stem .. **36**

19. Flowers and leaves appearing at different times on the same tuber or rootstock .. **20**

— Flowers and leaves contemporaneous or the pseudobulb and the new leaves developing during flowering time .. **21**

20. Tubers globular, usually first formed on underground runners; leaf solitary, heart-shaped, radiately plaited; sepals and petals linear or narrow-lanceolate, nearly of the same length. **Pogonia. p. 156.**

— Rootstock cylindrical, horizontal; leaves one or two, long-linear; sepals and petals unequal in length and shape. **Pachystoma. p. 74.**

21. Upper part of peduncle decurved, the corymbose inflorescence pendulous; sepals and petals nearly of the same length; the lip having the shape of a bowl with a long spout. **Geodorum. p. 111.**

— The whole of the flower-bearing axis erect **22**

22. Blade of leaf or leaves cordate at its base, not attenuated into the petiole or gradually passing into the leaf-sheath, ovate, orbicular or kidney-shaped in general outline **23**

— Leaf-blade contracted at its base into the leaf-stalk or continued downwards into the leaf-sheath. **24**

23. The single leaf rising from the same globular tuber as the two-flowered scape, broadly reniform in outline.
A species of **Pogonia. p. 156.**

— Leaves ovate, each terminating a spindle-shaped pseudobulb. **Nephelaphyllum. p. 76.**

24. Tubers or pseudobulbs globose; sepals and petals nearly equal **25**

— Tubers or pseudobulbs ovoid-oblong or spindle-shaped or absent **27**

25. Leaf ovate; inflorescence from the base of the pseudobulb; lip with a slender curved spur. **Tipularia. p. 95.**

— Leaf or leaves lanceolate or linear; inflorescence from the side or from near the top of the pseudobulb; lip not spurred .. **26**

26. Scape terminating in a raceme of 7 or more flowers; distance between the tip of the dorsal sepal and the tip of the lip 10—13 mm. **Oreorchis. p. 112.**

— Scape 3—4-flowered; distance between the tip of the dorsal sepal and the tip of the lip about 36 mm. **Spathoglottis. p. 74.**

27. Lower parts of sepals cohering into a tube or an urn-shaped structure .. 28

— Sepals either entirely free or the lateral sepals adnate along their neighbouring edges to the foot of the column forming a chin (or mentum) .. 29

28. Inflorescence slender, peduncle less than 5 mm. in thickness bearing a few distant bracts; raceme very lax, sometimes slightly branched; flowers forming a right or somewhat obtuse angle with the ovary, hanging downwards, 15—18 mm. long; lower part of sepals connate into a short cylindrical tube. **Anthogonium. p. 73.**

— Inflorescence stout, the peduncle rising from the lower part of a large ovoid pseudobulb, densely clothed with broad imbricate sheaths and ending in a corymb of a few fleshy flowers; sepals forming a ventricose, urn-shaped structure, the lateral sepals adnate to the long foot of the column and forming with it a large pouch; flowers 38—45 mm. long and 20 mm. in diameter. **Acanthephippium. p. 79.**

29. Flowers large, lateral sepals 35—80 mm. long.

Species of **Phajus. p. 77.**

— Flowers middle-sized, lateral sepals less than 30 mm. in length 30

30. Inflorescence a compound raceme; peduncle arising from the side of a large pear-shaped pseudobulb; flowers scattered; leaves several, linear.

A species of **Eulophia. p. 109.**

— Inflorescence a simple raceme or a densely crowded corymb **31**

31. Corymb or raceme densely flowered .. **32**

— Flowers not crowded, but forming a lax raceme **33**

32. Lip without side-lobes and spur; the creeping rhizome composed of links which at their outer ends terminate alternately in an inflorescence and in a single long-stalked oblong-lanceolate leaf. **Diglyphosa. p. 74.**

Lip with side-lobes and a narrow-cylindric spur; rhizome consisting of spindle-shaped ringed links producing at their thicker end a false stem made up of leaf-sheaths and at the base of the false stem a scape terminating in a dense corymb which finally lengthens into a short dense-flowered raceme. A species of **Calanthe. p. 102.**

33. Links of the creeping rootstock terminating in a single lanceolate or lanceolate-oblong leaf, the inflorescence either arising at the base of an ovoid-oblong or spindle-shaped pseudobulb or terminating successive links of a composite rootstock in alternation with a single leaf .. **34**

— Leaves several, either forming a false stem consisting of their sheaths or alternate on the upper part of a well-developed stem .. **35**

34. Inflorescence and leaf terminating alternately successive links of a composite rootstock, their bases at first only slightly swollen, but later on forming ovoid pseudobulbs tapering upwards; lip with two basal auricles; column with two opposite triangular teeth at the middle. **Chrysoglossum. p. 73.**

— Inflorescence arising at the base of a spindle-shaped or ovoid-oblong pseudobulb; lip not auricled; column without median teeth. **Tainia. p. 75.**

35. Inflorescence arising in the axil of a scale-like leaf-sheath some distance from the ground and below the leafy upper part of the stem; leaves large, elliptic-oblong; the base of the stem at first only slightly thickened, later on developing into a ovoid pseudo-bulb. A species of **Calanthe. p. 102.**

— Inflorescence either arising from the base of a false stem formed by the sheaths of several long-linear leaves or inserted on the slightly thickened base of a stem bearing upwards a few oblong-oblanceolate leaves and having at its base cylindric spongy roots. Species of **Cymbidium. p. 113.**

36. Flowers in axillary racemes or corymbs .. **37**

— Flowers in a terminal raceme on a leafy stem **38**

37. Raceme single, about 7-flowered, in the axil of the lowest leaf; peduncle decurved; flowers remote; sepals lanceolate-oblong; lip with side-lobes and spurred.
A species of **Phajus. p. 77.**

— Flowers in a number of axillary corymbose racemes much shorter than their leaves; peduncle short and straight; flowers close-set; sepals and petals oblanceolate, long-clawed; lip spoon-shaped, the basal part forming a long, linear handle. **Corymbis. p. 160.**

38. Lip either with two separate spurs or a deeply two-cleft spur **39**

Lip either without a true spur, sometimes saccate or gibbous at its base, or with a single undivided or only slightly cleft or lobed spur **41**

39. Spur two-cleft; stem decumbent at its basal part; tips of petals cohering; lip adpressed to the column, end-lobe small, transversely oblong, deflexed. **Physurus. p. 162.**

— Stem arising from an underground tuber; spurs two **40**

40. A small, one-leaved, one-flowered herb; leaf cordate; lip inferior, with two small, thin spurs at its base, basal part upright, embracing the column, apical lobe expanded with dentate margin, deflexed; dorsal sepal arching over the basal part of the lip; petals none. **Corysanthes. p. 158.**

— Stem with two or more lanceolate-oblong leaves; lip superior, hood-shaped, with two conical spurs; petals present **Satyrium. p. 194.**

41. Lower part of sepals united into a ventricose tube; flowers two or only one inserted near the top of the stem .. **42**

— Sepals free from each other; flowers usually more than two in a raceme .. **43**

42. End-lobe of lip entire, but fringed; leaves withered at flowing time. **Cheirostylis. p. 174.**

— End-lobe of lip two-cleft, not fringed; leaves fresh at flowering time, in one species greatly reduced. Species of **Zeuxine. p. 167.**

43. Stem decumbent at its lower part, then erect, never producing a pseudobulb .. **44**

— Stem rising straight up from the ground, either simply rooting at its base or arising from a tuber or a pseudobulb, or, if decumbent for a very short distance, then accompained by a pseudobulb .. **49**

44. Lip superior, nearly hemispheric; petals hammer-shaped. **Hetairia. p. 174.**

— Lip inferior **45**

45. Lip spurred, spur either long and slender or sack-like or globular **46**

Lip without any kind of spur, the basal part boat-shaped, bowl-shaped or scoop-shaped **47**

46. Spur long and slender; end-lobe of lip nearly square. **Herpysma. p. 161.**

— Spur sack- or pouch-shaped or globular; middle part of lip long and narrow, the edges rarely entire, in one case toothed, mostly each with a comb-like fringe, the end-lobe two-cleft or two-lobed. **Anoectochilus. p. 171.**

47. End-lobe of lip divided into two obovate, obtriangular, squarish or linear, more or less divergent lobes. **Zeuxine. p. 167.**

— End-lobe of lip entire **48**

48. End-lobe of lip linear, lanceolate, oblong, ovate or obtriangular either straight or recurved, revolute or reflexed, always conspicuous. **Goodyera. p. 163.**

— End-lobe of lip either squarish and fleshy or very small and with inflexed margins. Species of **Zeuxine. p. 167.**

49. Lip spurred, spur cylindric, conical, obovoid or globular.

— Lip without a spur of any kind, if saccate at its base, then entirely hidden by the sepals and petals **56**

50. Inflorescence and young leaves produced on an undeveloped pseudobulb, the latter as also the leaves fully developing only after flowering time; the sheaths of the leaves usually forming a false stem; the older pseudobulbs commonly arranged in a row; lip with side-lobes and an entire, fringed or bilobulate end-lobe. **Calanthe. p. 102.**

— Stem either directly rooting in the ground or with one or two tubers at its base; tubers irregularly cylindric or ellipsoidal or more or less globular, ovoid or obovoid **51**

51. Flowers not exceeding 4 mm. in length or diameter; spur correspondingly minute **52**

— Flowers more than 4 mm. in length or diameter **54**

52. Leaf solitary, stalked, ovate, rather less than 4 cm. long, inserted directly on a small ovoid pseudobulb at the side of the slender, thin peduncle. **Didiciea. p. 54.**

— Leaves inserted on the flower-bearing axis at various heights, solitary or two or several, leaf-blade usually directly passing into the leaf-sheath, mostly longer than 4 cm., ovate to lanceolate or oblanceolate .. **53**

53. Lip *either* trapezoidal in outline and with very shallow crenulate side-lobes *or* broadly ovate, nearly circular and concave and quite entire; flowering plant not exceeding 18 cm. in height, usually considerably shorter. Species of **Herminium. p. 190.**

— Lip *either* lanceolate and entire, about twice as long as broad, *or* relatively broader and distinctly three-lobes or three-cleft; leaves solitary *or* two or several; flowering plant usually more or considerably more than 15 cm. in height, rarely only 6—15 cm. high and then the lip superior. Species of **Habenaria. p. 177.**

54. Lip superior; lateral sepals connate along their inner edges; inflorescence a conical raceme, its peduncle bearing numerous linear spreading bracts; leaves two, nearly opposite, close to the inflorescence and longer than it, large, elliptical, plaited. A species of **Tropidia. p. 160.**

— Lip inferior; sepals free from each other; flowers few or forming a cylindrical or one-sided raceme; leaves solitary or two to several and manifestly alternate .. **55**

55. Lip *either* entire or nearly so and then broadly elliptic or nearly square, no more than one and a half times as long as broad; *or* three-lobed, the lobes either very short and blunt or oblong and with rounded or truncate ends, the mid-lobe entire *or* two-cleft; the spur stout cylindric or conical or stout- or slender-club-shaped; flowers purple, pinkish, or white, never green or yellowish.

Orchis. p. 175.

— Lip *either* entire with or without minute side-lobes, from two to five times as long as broad, ovate-oblong or lanceolate or linear, *or* three-lobed to three-partite, the mid-lobe usually several or many times as long as wide, the side-lobes filiform or variously divided or falcate or shorter but acute; *or* lip (in one species) deeply two-lobed; spur from globular to very slender-conical or slender-club-shaped; flowers entirely or in part of some green tint, more rarely entirely white, only in one species pink. **Habenaria. p. 177.**

56. The bases of successive leaf-blades separated by well-marked intervals, the number of leaves exceeding three .. **57**

— Leaves *either* solitary *or* two, opposite or with a short interval between their bases, *or* several closely crowded together .. **61**

57. Flowers in a terminal and a number of leaf-opposed, very short, cluster-like racemes; leaves lanceolate, many-nerved.
A species of **Tropidia. p. 160.**

— Raceme terminal, either simple or compound. **58**

58. Flowering plant 120—210 cm. (4—7 feet) in height; leaves linear, strap-shaped, recurved; flowers in a terminal panicle, very large; distance between the tip of the dorsal sepal and the tip of the lip 6—8 cm; lip of a brilliant rose-purple colour, its base convolute, its mouth oblique, the end-lobe nearly square, deeply two-cleft. **Arundina. p. 80.**

Flowering plant not exceeding 80 cm. in height; leaves lanceolate or ovate-oblong or elliptic; flowers in a terminal simple raceme, middle-sized; distance between tip of dorsal sepal and tip of lip not exceeding 3 cm; end-lobe of lip entire .. **59**

59. End-lobe of lip jointed to the trough- or bowl-shaped basal part; two globular swellings either near the outer end of the basal or near the inner part of the apical part of the lip. **Epipactis. p. 159.**

End-lobe of lip continuous with the basal part **60**

60\. Leaves ovate or elliptic-oblong 3—5 cm. broad; base of stem with two tubers; parts of the flowers spreading; lip lanceolate-oblong.
A variety of **Habenaria geniculata. p. 177.**

— Leaves lanceolate, up to 3 cm. in breadth curved backward sword-like; stem rising from a horizontal rhizome; lip concealed by the sepals and petals, basal part concave or saccate, apical part concave and strongly 3—4-ribbed. **Cephalanthera. p. 159.**

61\. Lip superior, ovary not twisted; flowering stem usually growing by the side of last season's cylindrical or ovoid-oblong pseudobulb; leaves ovate or elliptic-oblong, large. **Microstylis. p. 44.**

— Lip inferior **62**

62\. Leaves usually one or two, rarely as many as three **63**

— Leaves more than three **65**

63\. Lip linear or triangular-lanceolate, rarely broadly ovate; stem with one or two tubers at its base; leaves one to three, usually twice to many times as long as broad, linear, oblanceolate or oblong-elliptic; flowers in some species minute. Species of **Herminium. p. 190.**

— Lip transversely or longitudinally oblong or obovate or spathulate, pendulous or recurved **64**

64. Lip minutely apiculate at the truncate, rounded or retuse apical margin, flat or recurved to revolute; flowering plant either associated with or rising from a pseudobulb, leaves one or two, ovate-cordate or broadly linear-oblong or broad-lanceolate.
Species of **Liparis. p. 48.**

— Lip *either* transversely oblong with a fringe of coarse teeth *or* oblong with parallel sides and a short lanceolate end-lobe *or* elliptic-oblong, obovate or spathulate and more or less deeply cleft at its apex; leaves always in pairs, opposite or subopposite, broadly ovate or suborbicular; stem without tubers or pseudobulbs at or near its base. **Listera. p. 148.**

65. Leaves linear, clustered near the base of the stem, about 4—10 cm. long and 6 mm. and less in width; flowers 3—5 mm. across, white, sometimes pink.
Spiranthes. p. 162.

Leaves ovate, elliptic to broadly lanceolate, 10—20 cm. long, the larger ones about 4—7 cm. broad .. .. .. **66.**

66. Stem stout and fleshy; floral axis striated; petals linear with recurved margins; flowers brownish-purple.
A species of **Liparis. p. 48.**

— Floral axis slender rising from a false stem formed by the sheaths of the leaves, associated with pseudobulbs from a former flowering season; petals lanceolate; flowers light lavender-coloured.
Species of **Calanthe. p. 102.**

67. All the sepals connate into a tube to beyond their middle **68**

— Either all the sepals free from each other or only the lateral sepals connate at their base directly or through the foot of the column **69**

68. Pseudobulbs disc-shaped or depressed-spheroidal; leaves not exceeding 5 cm. in length; flowers solitary or in pairs, nearly sessile, dull red or brown. **Porpax. p. 80.**

— Pseudobulbs ovoid to cylindric; leaves exceeding 7 cm. in length; flowers many, forming a showy one-sided raceme, scarlet or yellow. **Cryptochilus. p. 102.**

69. Plant at flowering time or entirely without leaves; neither stem nor pseudobulbs **70**

— Plant with leaves at flowering time .. **71**

70. Raceme few-flowered, less than 2 cm. in length; flowers not exceeding 5 mm.; sepals and petals green. **Taeniophyllum. p. 144.**

— Raceme many-flowered, lax, 7—38 cm. long; flowers about 12 mm. across; parts of flower yellow, sepals and petals with brown spots, lip with brown bands.
A species of **Sarcochilus. p. 124.**

71. Leaves terete 72

— Leaves flat, rarely semiterete 77

72. Leaf terminal on a rush-like stem or branch; flowers less than 3 mm. long, forming a tiny cluster just below the base of the leaf; lip narrow-spathulate; column deeply bilobed; flowers white except the yellow end of the lip. **Ceratostylis. p. 145.**

Leaves several, lateral 73

73. Lip without a spur 74

Lip spurred 75

74. Lip inserted on the base of the footless column, consisting of a saccate or concave or flat basal part and a decurved end-lobe; flowers in extra-axillary small, shortly stalked clusters; sepals green. **Luisia. p. 121.**

— Lip inserted on the outer end of the foot of the column, fleshy, oblong; foot longer than the column; peduncle terminal, 2-5 cm. long, 1—4-flowered; sepals white-woolly outside, golden-brown on the upper surface. A species of **Eria. p. 81.**

75. Inflorescence and stem suberect; raceme 2—6-flowered on an extra-axillary peduncle; flowers 6—10 cm. across; sepals and petals rose-coloured, sometimes white. A species of **Vanda. p. 128.**

- Inflorescence pendulous or drooping on a pendulous or erect stem; flowers 2 cm. or ess ac oss 76

76. Flowers one or two, on a pendulous slender peduncle; spur not divided into two compartments; flowers white, spur pinkish. A species of **Aerides. p. 128.**

— Raceme of six or more flowers, pendulous or decurved; spur divided into two collateral compartments by a septum; sepals and petals buff-coloured with purplish markings or brown with edges and midrib yellowish, lip white, pink or lavender-coloured.
Two species of **Sarcanthus. p. 141.**

77. Epiphytes with typical pseudobulbs, pseudobulbs *either* single, ovoid to cylindric, *or* several joined end to end and marked off from each other by constrictions, *or* forming a branched system .. **78**

— Pseudobulbs absent or joined together end to end into a stem-like structure .. **98**

78. Pseudobulbs single, not several joined end to end **79**

— Several pseudobulbs joined end to end or forming a branch-system **95**

79. Lateral sepals *either* cohering all along their inner edges *or* connate both at base and apex but free between; scape arising from the base of the pseudobulb.
Ione. p. 207.

— Sepals entirely free from each other or only connate at their bases and free higher up **80**

80. Column not extended at its base into a "foot" 81

— "Foot" of column well developed .. 82

81. Sepals exceeding, and usually considerably exceeding 1 cm. in length **Coelogyne. p. 89.**

— Sepals not, or only slightly exceeding 1 cm. in length, in most species shorter .. 82

82. Inflorescence terminal on fully or partially developed pseudobulbs 83

— Inflorescence rising from the base of a pseudobulb 85

83. Pseudobulbs inserted at some distance from each other on a rhizome clothed with imbricate scales; peduncle bearing one or several sets of imbricate bracts below the terminal spike; flowers all turning to one and the same side.
A species of **Coelogyne. p. 89.**

— Pseudobulbs single or in clusters .. 84

84. Flowers globose, sepals concave, the lateral ones connate at their base; petals oblong; column short.
A species of **Pholidota. p. 91**

— Flowers open, lateral sepals free from each other, like the linear petals spreading; column rather elongated. **Liparis. p. 48**

85. Column elongated, about as long as the dorsal sepal; claw of the narrow-lanceolate lip bent in the form of an S; raceme pendulous, 5—8 flowered. **Panisea. p. 95.**

— Column shorter than sepals and lip **86**

86. Sepals connivent; sepals, petals and lip nearly parallel; inflorescence erect; petals linear or narrowly ovate. **Thelasis. p. 146.**

— Petals more or less spreading, either nearly semicircular or lanceolate with a broad basal part contracted into a narrow tapering apical part; flowers either solitary on a short slender stalk or many in a decurved raceme terminating an erect peduncle. **Sonapia. p. 208.**

87. Inflorescence either from the top of a pseudobulb or from among the leaves or leaf-opposed or from the axil of a scale **88**

— Scape arising from the base of a pseudobulb **89**

88. Pollinia 8, in two sets of four. **Eria. p. 81.**

— Pollinia 4. **Dendrobium. p. 54.**

89. Lateral sepals remote from the dorsal and much larger, attached to the middle of the long and curved foot of the column, connate with each other both at base and apex; lip jointed to the foot and mobile. **Monomeria. p. 98.**

Lateral sepals close to the dorsal .. **90**

90. Flowers less than 4 mm. in length or diameter **91**

— Flowers more, often considerably more than 4 mm. in length or diameter .. **92**

91. Leaves 10—15 cm. long; inflorescence much longer, raceme densely and many-flowered. **Phreatia. p. 147.**

— Leaves 2.5—3 cm. long; flowers solitary; pedicel shorter than the pseudobulb. A species of **Bulbophyllum. p. 197.**

92. Pseudobulbs bearing three or more large leaves, compressed, 7—10 cm. long, vertically furrowed, covered with large furrowed leaf-sheaths, inserted on a stout rhizome clothed with imbricating tubular scales; inflorescence erect, axis stout, flowers forming a lax raceme. A species of **Eria. p. 81.**

— Pseudobulbs bearing one or two leaves, discoid, ovoid, or cylindric, usually quite bare of scales, or entirely absent .. **93**

93. Inflorescence hanging straight down from the base of the pseudobulb, its axis rigid, 4—5 mm. thick near its base and bearing a somewhat lax raceme of at least 15 middle-sized and yellowish-green purplish-brown—spotted and—streaked flowers; leaf erect, solitary, blade 15—24 cm. long on a stout, 7—14 cm. long petiole; apical lobe of lip tongue-shaped, deeply grooved. **Acrochaene. p. 99.**

— Peduncle *either* erect and terminating in a single or a pair of flowers or in a head, umbel, or an erect or nodding raceme, *or* pendulous, about 1 mm. thick and terminating in an umbel or a short raceme **94**

94. Lateral sepals twice or several times as long as very rarely somewhat less than twice as long as the dorsal sepal, often more or less cohering, as a rule in consequence of a twist, by the edges which in bud are adjacent to the dorasl sepal, sometimes produced into a long filament. **Cirrhopetalum. p. 67.**

— Lateral sepals mostly about as long as the dorsal, more rarely one and a half times as long, usually free from each other, sometimes more or less cohering along the edges which are in bud adjacent to each other. **Bulbophyllum. p. 197.**

95. Pseudobulbous stem strictly erect, rooting at its very base; flowers inserted all round **96**

— Pseudobulbous stem or the pseudobulbs which form branches on a rhizome emitting roots at least at the lower joints, more or less horizontal or pendulous; flowers in two rows **97**

96. Stem clavate; leaves crowded near the top; raceme pendulous, 15—25 cm. long; flowers very many, densely crowded, 2.5 to 4 cm. across.
A species of **Dendrobium. p. 54.**

— Lowest internode the thickest; leaves arising from the successive joints of the upper internodes; inflorescences shorter than their leaves, few-flowered; flowers 1 cm. and less across. **Tylostylis. p. 89.**

97. Sepals connivent or suberect, never widely spreading; flowers 1 cm. and less across; column short and stout, winged both on top and the sides. **Pholidota. p. 96.**

— Sepals, petals and lip widely spreading; column long and slender, winged only at the sides. **Otochilus. p. 95.**

98. Lip with a cylindrical or funnel-shaped or pouch-shaped spur **99**

— Lip without a spur, or the side-lobes of the lip united with their lower halves into a bowl-shaped structure **115**

99. Spur remote from the base of the lip .. **100**

— Spur situated at the base of the lip .. **101**

100. Stem hardly any; leaves 7—15 cm. long and 4—5 cm. broad, broadly oblong; lip much longer than the sepals; spur at the junction of the basal and apical parts of the lip, rectangularly bent; lateral lobules of the end-lobe with a comb-like fringe of lanceolate teeth. **Ornithochilus. p. 121.**

— Stem stout, woody; leaves 15—24 cm. long and 1.2 cm. broad, linear-oblong; lip shorter than the sepals; spur between the base of the lip and a large papilla just behind the apical part, recurved; end-lobe not fringed. A species of **Archnanthe. p. 125.**

101. Stem repeatedly dichotomously branched, pendulous, densely covered with scarious sheaths, each branch bearing a terminal 1—2-flowered short peduncle and a subterminal fleshy lanceolate leaf; flower 6 mm. long. **Ritaia. p. 100**

— Stem never dichotomously branched, in most cases not branched at all; leaves forming a rosette or inserted at intervals along the stem **102**

102. Inflorescence subterminal; stem erect, but raceme drooping; upper leaves crowded close to the base of the peduncle; flowers large; lip thimble-shaped with an oblique shell-like mouth
A species of **Phajua. p. 77**

— Inflorescence axillary or extra-axillary, not terminal **103**

103. Spur (Pseudospur) formed by the two-lobed basal parts of the lip in combination with the long foot of the column, the spur either a chort conical sac or an irregular cone; roots flat. **Doritis. p. 120.**

— Spur formed by a cylindrical, conical or pouch-like protrusion of the basal part of the lip **104**

104. Lip consisting for the greater part of a pouch-shaped or narrowly funnel-shaped spur, the side- and end-lobes being minute or obscure **105**

— Either the end-lobe of the lip or its side-lobes or both more or less conspicuous, never both of them minute or obsolete **106**

105. The cavity of the spur not divided into compartments; lips jointed to the curved foot of the short and stout column; spur narrowly and irregularly funnel-shaped, bulbous at its tip; inflorescences as long as or longer than the pendulous strap-shaped leaves. **Ornitharium. p. 143.**

— The cavity of the spur narrowed by two swellings (calli) and more or less completely divided by a septum into two longitudinal chambers; column twisted, not extended into a foot; inflorescences shorter than the narrow-lanceolate leaves. **Camarotis. p. 140.**

106. Sepals and petals narrow-lanceolate, long-acuminate, about 3 cm. long; peduncle leaf-opposed, upwards beset with two rows of small persistent floral bracts; stem erect, rigid, bearing 6—8 linear-oblong leaves and emitting numerous roots. **Dendrocolla. p. 143.**

— Sepals elliptic, oblanceolate, oblong or linear, rounded or obtuse at the tip .. **107**

107. Cavity of the spur more or less completely closed by two opposite or subopposite swellings of the wall (calli), either near its mouth or lower down .. **108**

— Spur-cavity continuous, neither contracted by swellings nor more or less divided into two compartments by a longitudinal septum **111**

108. Spur-cavity more or less completely divided into two compartments by longitudinous septa . .. **109**

— Spur cavity not divided into two longitudinal compartments **110**

109. The two swellings situated at the mouth of the spur; septum anterior-posterior dividing the spur-cavity into two equal collateral compartments; spur short and stout; lateral sepals ovate or obovate-oblong. **Sarcanthus. p. 141.**

— The two swellings situated about the middle of the spur; spur-cavity divided into two unequal anterior-posterior compartments by a plate inserted on the anterior callus; spur funnel-shaped, conical part elongated; lateral sepals linear-oblong. **Cleisocentron. p. 136.**

110. Stem either elongate or hardly any; inflorescences leaf-opposed. **Cleisostoma. p. 137.**

Stem short and stout; racemes extra axillary, but not leaf-opposed. **Stereochilus. p. 140.**

111. Inflorescence 15—35 cm. long; flowers very many, crowded into a dense cylindrical raceme as long as, or longer than the peduncle **112**

— Inflorescence less than 15 cm. in length; flowers in racemes, corymbs or clusters **114**

112. Inflorescence leaf-opposed or from below the leaves, pendulous; peduncle straight; lip consisting mainly of the wide-mouthed, funnel-shaped spur, with the lower part much curved forwards and ending in a bulbous tip; side-lobes small, sitting on the edge of the mouth of the spur, end-lobe with three lobules directed backwards and upwards.
A species of **Saccolabium. p. 130.**

— Inflorescence axillary or supra-axillary; peduncle decurved **113**

113. Spur forming a compressed, wide and deep pouch; lip without side-lobes; end-lobe obovate, acute, concave, with erect margins. **Rhynchostylis. p. 127.**

— Spur conical; lip either triangular with erose margins or with shallow side-lobes and a short linear end-lobe. **Aerides. p. 126.**

114. End-lobe of lip linear or ovate-oblong, subtruncate at the apex, trough-shaped or deeply grooved, upper surface either uniformly covered with bead-like protuberances (caruncles) or with four to six smooth or carunculate ridges, near its apex with or without two small knobs; lower part of stem densely covered with the remains of leaf-sheaths truncate at their projecting outer ends; flowers mostly large. 2.5—5 cm. across, in one species only 1.5 cm. across; spur funnel-shaped or short- and wide-conical. **Vanda. p. 128.**

— End-lobe of lip of various shapes, hardly ever oblong or caruncualate; lower part of stem only in one species densely covered with the remains of old leaf-sheaths; flowers never large; spur of various shapes, in some species funnel-shaped, in others thimble-shaped, bowl-shaped, hemispherical, pouch-shaped, cylindrical, conical, either straight, or incurved or **S**-shaped, tip acute, blunt or bulbous. **Saccolabium. p. 130.**

115. Sepals not exceeding 1 cm. in length, often considerably shorter **116**

— Sepals 1 cm. long or longer **127**

116. The leafless inflorescences rising directly from a creeping rhizome; leaves single, sessile or stalked borne on the same rhizome alternately with the inflorescences. **Bulbophyllum. p. 197.**

— Inflorescences or single flowers inserted on leafy stems or branches.

117. Flowers in heads or dense clusters .. **118**

— Flowers solitary or in loose clusters or in few—or many-flowered racemes .. **120**

118. Stem creeping, emitting elongated compressed pseudobulbs, bearing clusters of 3–4 leaves and in the axils of some of them on very short and thin peduncles heads of minute flowers, the heads 10—13 mm. in diameter.

A species of **Dendrobium. p. 54.**

— Flower- and leaf-bearing stems erect .. **119**

119. Flowers 10 mm. across, yellow marked with red. A species of **Eria. p. 81.**

— Flowers 5—6 mm. across, white. **Agrostophyllum. p. 99.**

120. Flowers minute, 0.5—2.5 mm. long, inserted on a fleshy or thin floral axis and forming a many-flowered terminal spike; leaves fleshy, riding, arranged in two rows. **Oberonia. p. 36.**

— Flowers 3—15 mm. across, solitary or a few forming lateral or terminal clusters or short racemes **121**

121. Leaves very numerous in two rows along the greater part of the stem .. **122**

— Leaves comparatively few, scattered or in clusters **124**

122. Upper surface of lip with a superposed horse-shoe-shaped appendage; lateral pair of sepals adnate to the long foot of the column and forming with it a chin (mentum). **Appendicula. p. 146.**

— Upper surface of lip without an appendage **123**

123. Lateral sepals adnate at their base to the long foot of the column and forming with it a chin; lip gradually narrowed down to its base.
Two species of **Dendrobium. p. 54.**

— Lateral sepals united directly by their basal edges thus forming a wide pouch; lip with a gibbous base. **Podochilus. p. 144.**

124. Side-lobes of the lip adnate to the foot of the column, their lower halves united into a two-grooved pouch, the upper halves free and pointing forward; end-lobe consisting of an obscure thickening; stem short, pendulous. **Sarcochilus. p. 124.**

— Side-lobes of lip not forming a pouch .. **125**

125. Stem hardly any; leaves 3—4 close together; foot of column at right-angles to it, short; the fleshy lip parallel to the column. **Biermannia. p. 120.**

— Stem more or less elongate, erect, pendulous or creeping **126**

126. Lip adnate to the base and slightly to the sides of the column, basal part trough-shaped, apical part triangular ending in two tails; inflorescence of 3—4 flowers. **Diploprora. p. 123.**

— Lip jointed to the long or short foot of the column. Species of **Eria. p. 81.**

127. Column extended at its base into a foot; lip inserted on the foot **128**

— Lip directly inserted on the base of the column, the column not extended into a foot **130**

128. Foot of column with two oblong erect lobes or two short horns; apical lobe of lip reniform or arrow-shaped, at its base *either* a semi-circular erose disc with two superposed processes each divided into two awns *or* a few backward-directed bristles. **Phalaenopsis. p. 119.**

— Foot of column entire **129**

129. Pollinia 4. **Dendrobium. p. 54.**

— Pollinia 8, in two sets of four. **Eria. p. 81.**

130. Inflorescence arising from the axils of leaves or leaf-sheaths **131**

— Inflorescence extra-axillary or leaf-opposed; sepals and petals fleshy or leathery **132**

131. Stem short, compressed; leaf-sheaths densely crowded and usually imbricated, in two opposite rows; leaves linear, very long; inflorescence elongated. **Cymbidium. p. 113.**

— Stem stout, elongated, lower part closely covered by old leaf-sheaths, their upper ends projecting and truncate; leaves broad-linear; flowers solitary or in very short two-flowered racemes, nodding. A species of **Vanda. p. 128.**

132. Stem 20—40 cm. long, erect; flowers rather less than 4 cm. across; sepals and petals wavy, white flushed with pink on both surfaces; apical part of lip laterally compressed. **Stauropsis. p. 124.**

— Stem 60 cm. long and longer, pendulous; flowers 4—8 cm. across; sepals and petals flat, white on the outer surface, upper surface with yellow and brown cross-bars or -lines; apical part of lip expanded, flat or the edges turned up. **Arachnanthe. p. 125.**

KEY TO THE SPECIES.

OBERONIA, Lindley.

1. Peduncle adnate to the side of a leaf or arising from about the middle of a leaf .. **2**

— Peduncle free from a neighbouring leaf, either axillary or terminal **3**

2. Peduncle compressed, adnate to a neighbouring leaf for the greater part of its length; floral axis straight or slightly bent, thick and fleshy, awl-shaped; flowers minute, sunk in pits of the floral axis, about 1 mm. long, not whorled, pale-brown; lip elliptic-oblong, not lobed. 2—4,000′; also from Garhwal to Khasia.
O. pachyrrhachis, Reichenbach fil.

— Inflorescence arising from about the middle of the uppermost leaf, decurved; floral axis nearly cylindric, fleshy; flowers 1.5 mm. long, arranged in numerous whorls, brown; lip roughly orbicular in outline, three-lobed, basal lobes coarsely pectinate, with a nectar-secreting elliptic cavity between them; end-lobe shortly obovate, nearly truncate.

Tista valley, 1.000′; also Khasia.
O. Jenkinsiana, Griffith.

3. The longer leaves all curved in the same direction, linear-ensiform, up to 50 cm. long; inflorescence somewhat shorter than the longest leaves, increasing in thickness upwards and only little less in diameter near the upper end than in the middle; flowers pale-brown; sepals and petals triangular; lip with two broad and rounded basal lobes, a squarish middle piece bearing two blister-like projections and a reniform bilobulate end-lobe, the lobules separated by a squarish gap; most parts of the lip hairy.

Tista valley, 1,500′ (?) ; also Khasia and Nilgiris. XI. **O. ensiformis,** Lindley.

— Leaves either straight or, if ensiform or falcate, then curved in various directions according to their position 4

4. Stem conspicuously flexuose, up to 15 cm. long; leaves ensiform to falcate, 2.5—8 cm. long and 5—8 mm. broad; inflorescence straight, about as long as the stem and 3—4 times as long as the longest leaf; flowers 1.2 mm. long, in slightly remote whorls, yellowish-green; sepals ovate; petals linear-oblong; lip broadly oblong in outline with small triangular side-lobes and a bifid end-lobe, the segments lanceolate, and separated by a narrow-triangular gap.

Chungthang, 6,000′. VIII.

O. falcata, King and Pantling.

— Stem straight or slightly curved, never flexuose, not more than 5 cm. long, often much shorter 5

5. Inflorescence gradually increasing in diameter from its base to its very tip; tip markedly truncate, about 5 mm. across; the spike either erect or flexuose or recurved; stem very short; leaves oblong or lanceolate to linear, 1—8 cm. long; flowers very many, about 1.3 mm. long, in close-set whorls, red-brown; sepals ovate, reflexed; petals elliptic and dentate; lip three-lobed, side-lobes obliquely ovate and denticulate, end-lobe larger, nearly square, shallowly emarginate, erose.

Tropical valleys. **O. demissa,** Lindley.

— Spike tapering to the acute tip either from the very base or from some point higher up, never truncate at the apex .. **6**

6. Spike straight or nearly so **7**

— Spike strongly recurved or overhanging **13**

7. Inflorescence 5 or more times as long as the longest leaf; leaves 2 cm. and less long, falcately ovate-oblong; flowers about 1.3 mm. long, brown, in whorls below, scattered near the upper end of the spike; sepals revolute; petals spreading and serrate; lip ovate-oblong, irregularly serrate, base truncate, with a round nectarial pit.

Tista valley, near Sivoke, 1,000′; also Perak. IV, V.

O. Prainiana, King and Pantling.

Inflorescence not more than two and a half times as long as the longest leaf .. 8

8. Flowers either scattered along the axis of the spike or arranged in whorls with clearly defined interstices between themselves 9

— Flowers densely crowded, either not whorled at all or the whorls without intervals between themselves .. 11

9. Flowers in well-defined whorls right up to the tip of the spike, 0.9 mm. long; stem less than 1 cm. long; sepals spreading; petals recurved; lip consisting of a basal fleshy reniform and an apical thinner transversely elliptic erose part.

Tendong, 6,000′. VII.

O. micrantha, King and Pantling.

— Flowers not whorled at all or not whorled towards the apex, 1.25 mm. long; stem 2—5 cm. long; petals not recurved; end-lobe of lip bifid or two-lobed .. 10

10. Sepals and petals spreading; petals broadly lanceolate, quite entire; lip with two obliquely ovate and falcate side-lobes and a much longer narrowly oblong deeply two-cleft end-lobe, the segments caudate-acuminate, nearly parallel and separated by a narrow-oblong gap; flowers red-brown, in whorls except near the apex of the spike.

6,000′ common; also Nipal and Khasia. VII, VIII.

O. caulescens, Lindley.

— Lateral sepals spreading, dorsal sepal and the petals erect; petals narrow-oblong, erose; lip without lateral lobes, end-lobe with a narrow truncate base, widening upwards and divided into two diverging oblong obtuse lobules separated by a trapezoidal gap; flowers not in whorls, forming a very lax and narrow spike.

Sureil and Rungbi, 6,000′. V.

O. auriculata, King and Pantling.

11. Leaves lanceolate, none longer than 25 mm.; spike shortly spindle-shaped or conical; floral bracts as long as the ovary, oblong-lanceolate; flowers not whorled, 1.5 mm. long; sepals and petals translucent, the petals pale-yellow; lip red-brown, three-lobed, lateral lobes short, end-lobe oblong in outline, deeply bifid, segments separated by an oblong, broad gap.

Tista valley, at Guru Bathan, 1,500′. II.

O. parvula, King and Pantling.

— Leaves linear or linear-oblong, the longer ones usually longer than 25 mm. long; spike cylindrical or very narrowly long-conical; at least the lower floral bracts projecting beyond the flowers; flowers whorled, but the whorls closely crowded; all parts of the flowers reddish-brown .. **12**

12. Leaves fleshy, linear and more or less falcate, about 2—5 cm. long; spike thin; floral bracts ovate-lanceolate, longer than the flowers; lip with two linear-oblong side-lobes and an obcordate end-lobe, the lobules separated by a shallow gap; the nectary forming a median tunnelled ridge.

5—9,000′; also Khasia and Naga Hills. VI—XI. **O. obcordata,** Lindley.

— Leaves flaccid, linear-oblong, nearly straight, about 2—13 cm. long; spike cylindric, rather thick; lower floral bracts ovate ending in a long thread-like tail; lip narrow-obovate in outline, deeper in colour, with two basal thread-like segments and a deeply two-cleft end-lobe, the terminal segments being separated by a deep, narrowly trapezoidal gap.

Base of hills; also Burma.

O. rufilabris, Lindley.

13. Spike very densely flowered, the flowers often whorled, always very numerous .. **14**

— Spike laxly flowered, flowers not in whorls, always with a clear interstice between neighbouring ones .. **17**

14. Longer leaves not exceeding 5 cm.; peduncle terete **15**

— Longer leaves more than 5 cm. long; sometimes as much as 25 cm. **16**

15. Flowers about 0.5 mm. long; in well defined whorls, the whorls being very close-set except near the upper end of the spike; sepals and petals broad-ovate; lip not much longer, but broader, nearly orbicular in outline, with a shallow depression at the base, three-lobed, basal lobes small, end-lobe large, erose, with a small triangular apical incision.

At Namgah, 6,000′. IX.

O. emarginata, King and Pantling.

— Flowers about 1.2 mm. long, not whorled, reddish-brown; sepals ovate-cordate; petals oblong; lip with two narrow denticulate side-lobes and a bilobulate and end-lobe; the lobules oblong, blunt, separated by an oblong gap.

Bhotan Frontier, banks of Jaldaka river, 900 in. X. **O. Croftiana,** King and Pantling.

16. The longer leaves no more than 15 mm. broad; peduncle terete, rather densely covered with linear bracts; flowers brown, 2.5 mm. long; lip with broadly oblong side-lobes and a large deeply cleft end-lobe, the lobules broad-oblong separated by a triangular gap.

Valleys 3—4,000′, common; also Khasia and Naga Hills. X—XII.

O. myriantha, Lindley.

— The larger leaves up to 25 cm. long, broadly ensiform; peduncle winged, not bearing bracts; flowers 1.5 mm. long, pale-green or yellow; lip orbicular in outline, side-lobes pectinate, end-lobe transversely oblong, deeply emarginate, coarsely erose.

Tropical valleys, common; also Assam, Burma and Andamans. IX—XII.

O. iridifolia, Lindley.

17. Floral axis 3—4 mm. thick, fleshy; leaves fleshy, lanceolate-ovate, 12—25 mm. long, 5—13 mm. broad; flowers 1 mm. long; sepals and petals ovate, spreading, pale reddish-brown; lip deeper coloured, about as long, broad-ovate, side-lobes very

narrow, erose, end-lobe nearly semicircular, entire.

Base of hills near Siliguri, 900′; very rare. II.

O. pachyphylla, King and Pantling.

— Floral axis slender, about 1 mm. thick; flowers green or yellow **18**

18. Stem hardly any; flowers green; sepals and petals reflexed **19**

— Stem 5—8 cm. long; leaves linear, somewhat ensiform; flowers yellow, 1.5 mm. long; sepals ovate, petals oblong, both spreading; lip much longer, side-lobes resembling basal auricles, end-lobe oblong below, deeply bifid upwards, segments obliquely lanceolate, acute, separated by a triangular gap with a truncate base.

Song-chong-la, 6,000′; Namgah, 5,000′. VII. **O. longilabris,** King and Pantling.

19. Inflorescence about twice as long as the longest leaf; raceme nearly pendulous; peduncle winged; flowers 2 mm. long; lip about twice as long as the sepals, trapezoidal in outline, irregularly dentate with two roundish apical lobules separated by a squarish gap.

Tropical valleys, 1,000′; very rare. X.

O. lobulata, King and Pantling.

— Inflorescence about as long as the longest leaf; raceme decurved; peduncle not winged; flowers 1.5 mm. long; lip more than twice as long as the sepals, basal part nearly square, apical part deeply cleft into two somewhat falcate divergent lobules separated by a triangular broad gap.

Tista valley, 1,000′; also Khasia and Manipur. X. **O. pyrulifera,** Lindley.

MICROSTYLIS, Nuttall.

1. Stem leafless, bearing only a few scales .. **2**

— Stem leafy **3**

2. Tuber globular, about 9 mm. in diameter; flowering plant 7—15 cm. high; raceme 2.5—5 cm. long; floral bracts erect; flowers greenish; sepals ovate, dorsal reflexed; lateral sepals and the linear petals revolute; lip elliptic in outline, with basal erect short lobes.

Chungthang, 6,000′; Lachen valley. VII.
M. aphylla, King and Pantling.

— Tuber oblong, about 2 cm. long; flowering plant 17—24 cm. high; raceme about 12 cm. long; floral bracts reflexed; flowers yellowish flushed with purple; sepals elliptic, dorsal with revolute margins, lateral recurved; petals linear resting on the lateral sepals; lip ovate in outline, with two basal, broadly falcate lobes.

Tista valley, 1,000′. VI.
M. aphylla, King and Pantling.

3. Spike dense, flowers closely packed .. **4**

— Spike more or less lax, always at least a small clear space between successive flowers **5**

4. Leaf solitary, oblong-elliptic, blade 3.7—10 cm. long, blunt; inflorescence narrow—cylindric, about 6 mm. in diameter; flowers about 4 mm. long, yellowish-green; sepals ovate; petals lanceolate; lip broad-ovate, with thickened margins, produced into a fleshy point, a raised line running along the middle.

Lachen valley, 12,000′, Chumbi valley; also Nipal to Simla. VII.
M. cylindrostachya, Reichenbach fil.

— Leaves 3—6, broadly lanceolate, blade 7—30 cm. long, 1.8—13 cm. broad, acute; inflorescence stout-cylindric, about 2 cm. in diameter; flowers 6 mm. long, red or yellow; sepals oblong, lateral falcate; petals linear; lip scoop-shaped, lateral lobes broad, end-lobe short, ovate.

600—25,000′; also Paresnath, Khasia, Manipur, Burma, and elsewhere.
M. congesta, Reichenbach fil.

5. Leaves 2, one broadly elliptic, the other ovate-lanceolate, length of blade 2.5—6.5 cm. neither plaited nor wavy; spike below scarcely 1 cm. across, very slender; flowers about 4 mm. long, yellowish-green; sepals lanceolate-oblong, longer than the linear petals; lip nearly circular, with thick obscure basal lobes and a narrowly lanceolate tip.

Lachen valley, 8—10,000′, common; westwards to Kashmir. **M. muscifera,** Ridley.

— Leaves 3—5, rarely only 2, ovate or elliptic-oblong, usually plaited and with a wavy margin, 7.5—13 cm. long; spike below at least 1.5 cm. across; flowers 8—14 mm. from tip of dorsal sepal to tip of lip ... 6

6. Lip deeply cup- or scoop-shaped .. 7

— Lip shallow or flat 8

7. Flowers only 2 or 3 open at the same time, 12—19 mm. in diameter; sepals broad-ovate, recurved; petals linear-oblong, recurved; lip forming a deep cup, basal auricles short, overlapping; colour of the flower ochre-yellow shaded with brown or yellow, with red blotches near the column.

1,500—3,000′.

M. Josephiana, Reichenbach fil.

— Flowers numerous, green, 5 mm. in diameter; sepals oblong with recurved margin, like the linear petals reflexed, lip scoop-shaped, with large erect side-lobes and a thickened triangular very short tip. Mangpu, 2—4,000′; also Jaintia Hills. VII.

M. Maximowicziana, King and Pantling.

8. Sepals concave, ovate, like the linear truncate petals purple; lip yellowish, concave, with two falcate converging and overlapping basal, and a transversely oblong shorter apical lobe; leaves of a shining greyish-green colour flushed with purple.

3—6,000′, common; also Jaintia Hills. VII—X. **M. khasiana,** Hooker fil.

— Sepals and petals revolute or their margins recurved 9

9. Basal lobes of the greenish-yellow lip obliquely lanceolate and converging, end lobe triangular; sepals and petals revolute, purple; leaves dark-green and purple with a paler border suffused with purple and dotted green.

Tista valley, 1,000—2,500′. VII—IX.

M. callosa, Reichenbach fil.

— Basal lobes of lip semi-ovate or falcate, end-lobe semi-elliptic or narrow-oblong; leaves, green or discoloured **10**

10. Inner edges of basal lobes parallel, showing the strongly recurved dorsal petal between them; edges of the semi-elliptical end-lobe continuous with the edges of the basal lobes, the end-lobe slightly notched; flowers yellowish-green; margin of leaves conspicuously undulate.

5—7,000′; westwards to Simla, also in Khasia and Ceylon. VI—IX.

M. Wallichii, Lindley.

— Basal lobes of lip falcate, converging or overlapping; end-lobe narrow-oblong, separated from the basal lobes by a shallow triangular incision and divided into two oblong rounded lobules about half-way down; flowers varying from pale-yellow to dull-purple; margin of leaves little or not at all wavy.

Tropical valleys below 5,000′; also Nipal and Khasia.

M. biloba, Lindley.

LIPARIS.

1. Terrestrial 2

— Epiphytic 9

2. Leaf solitary 3

— Leaves two or more 4

3. Leaf broadly ovate, 5—13 cm. long, 3—10 cm. broad, cordate; inflorescence about as long as the leaf; flowers green; lip obtriangular.
5—6,000′; also N.-W. Himalaya and Khasia. X, XI. **L. cordifolia,** Hooker fil.

— Leaf linear-oblong; 5—10 cm. long; 1.5—2.5 cm. broad; inflorescence longer than the leaf; flowers green except the purple olive-green-edged oblong, deflexed lip.
Chumbi valley, 11,000′; also Kumaon and Garhwal. **L. Glossula,** Reichenbach fil.

4. Flowering plant 10 cm. high and more .. 5

— Flowering plant not more than 6 cm. high; leaves 2, ovate or elliptic, about 13 mm. long; inflorescence with 2 to 3 yellowish flowers; lip oblong-obovate.
Below Jongri, 13,000′. VI.
L. pygmaea, King and Pantling.

5. Leaves 2, rarely 3 6

— Leaves 4—5, ovate-oblong, plicate, 10—20 cm. long; stem 20—25 cm. high; inflorescence much longer than the leaves; flowers brownish-purple; lip oblong, deflexed and revolute.

At Chungtang. 6,000′ and in the Lachen valley; also Kumaon, Nipal and Khasia. VI, VII. **L. bituberculata,** Lindley.

6. Leaves suborbicular, broadly ovate or elliptic-oblong, ½ as broad to nearly as broad as long 7

— Leaves elliptic-lanceolate, about 13 cm. long and ⅓ as broad; flowers few, green except the dull-purple quadrate lip.

Tropical valleys up to 6,000′; also Kumaon, the Naga Hills, Khasia, N.-E. Bengal, S. India and Burma. VII—IX.

L. paradoxa, Reichenbach fil.

7. Flowers yellow; stem springing from a cylindric root-bearing tuber accompanied by a rootless tuber, but pseudo-bulbs absent; leaves tapering to base and apex, ovate oblong, plicate, 7-nerved, 15—18 cm. long; less than half as broad; lip orbicular-reniform.

At Goke 2,000′ (and near Darjiling). VIII.

L. deflexa, Hooker fil.

– Flower green and purple; pseudobulbs present 8

8. Leaves elliptic, acute, with 3 pairs of lateral nerves and undulate margin, 2—6 cm. long, $\frac{1}{2}$ to $\frac{2}{3}$ as broad; sepals, petals and upper part of column green, greater part of lip and base of column purple, outer edge ot lip yellowish-green.

Lachen valley, 7,000′; also at elevations between 8—10,000′. **L. Cathcartii,** Hooker fil.

— Leaves broadly ovate to nearly orbicular, abruptly acute or short-acuminate with 5 pairs of lateral nerves, the flat elliptic lip and the petals purple, other parts of the flower green.

Sikkim 3,500—5,000′, common; also Nipal and Khasia. V. **L. nepalensis,** Lindley.

9. Leaf solitary **10**

— Leaves two or more **14**

10. Leaf elliptic or elliptic-oblong, 7-nerved, 2.5 to 10 cm. long, about half as broad, margin minutely wavy; inflorescence lax; flowers dark green except the brownish-purple margin of the broadly elliptic lip and its branching strongly marked nerves.

Sureil, Senchal, Rangbi, 6,000—6,500′. VI. **L. Gamblei,** Hooker fil.

— Leaf linear-lanceolate or oblanceolate .. **11**

11. Pseudobulb narrow-oblong, 6—7 cm. long, $\frac{1}{5}$ to $\frac{1}{3}$ as thick near the base, bearing a linear-oblong or oblanceolate, 12—25 cm. long and 2.5—3 cm. broad leaf; flowers pale brown, 15 mm. long; lip oblong.

Sureil, 4,000′; also in Bhotan and the Khasia Hills. VIII. **L. bhotanensis,** Griffith.

— Pseudobulbs crowded or tufted, ovoid or ellipsoid, 1.3 to 2 cm. long; flowers green or yellowish-green, less than 5 mm. long **12**

12. Inflorescence erect: flowers pale green, about 3 mm. long **13**

— Inflorescence overhanging; leaf linear-lanceolate, acute, 12—18 cm. long, about one-tenth as broad: flowers uniformly yellowish-green, between 4 and 5 mm. long; lip three-lobed.

Base of range east of the Jaldaga river, 800′ XII. **L. Mannii.**

13. Petals shorter than the sepals; lip broadly oblong, recurved from the middle; flowering plant 12—18 cm. high.

4—7,000′; also Khasia and Sunda Islands. **L. pusilla,** Ridley.

— Petals longer than the sepals; lip square, reflexed from the base; flowering plant 5—8 cm. high.

Tista Valley, 1,000′; also Kumaon. **L. Duthiei,** Hooker fil.

14. Inflorescence upright, sometimes flexuose **15**

— Inflorescence overhanging .. **19**

15. Flowering plant not exceeding 12 cm. in height; leaves three or more from the top of the ovoid-oblong pseudobulb, 2.5 cm. and less long; flowers yellow: lip quadrate, deflexed, deeply grooved.

6—8,000′. **L. perpusilla,** Hooker fil.

— Flowering plant 20 cm. high and often considerably higher; leaves two on each pseudobulb; flowers green or yellowish-green **16**

16. Leaves 5 to 10 cm. long, elliptic-oblong or elliptic-lanceolate, rising from the top of a stem-like, 7—15 cm. long pseudobulb; flowers in a rather dense raceme; lip quadrate-oblong, sharply recurved.

5—7,000′; also Khasia and Tenasserim. VII, VIII.

L. bistriata, Parish and Reichenbach fil.

— Leaves longer than 10 cm. **17**

17. Pseudobulbs oblong or ovoid, 2.5 to 4.5 cm. long; leaves oblanceolate gradually attenuated towards the base, 12 to 25 cm. long; flowers numerous, forming a rather dense raceme, about 8 mm. across; lip broadly obtriangular.

Pemiongtchi, 5,000′. XI.

L. Griffithii, Ridley.

— Pseudobulbs large, 5—15 cm. long .. **18**

18. Pseudobulbs narrowly ovoid-oblong, 5 to 8 cm. long; pseudo-stem formed of 4 to 5 large, ovate, imbricate sheaths; peduncle about equal to the raceme in length; flowers 1.8 to 2.5 cm. long; lip large, sub-orbicular.

1—2,000′; also Upper Assam, the Naga Hills and Khasia. VI to VIII.

L. plantaginea, Lindley

— Pseudobulbs cylindric and stem-like, close together in a row, 8—15 cm. long; raceme twice as long as peduncle; flowers about 6 mm. long: lip broadly oblong.
L. longipes, Lindley.

(*a*) Leaves 10—15 cm. long; 18 mm. broad; scape without bracts. *var.* **typica.**

Tropical Himalaya from Kumaon to Bhotan, 1—5.000′; also from Khasia to Perak, and Nilgiris and Ceylon. X—XII.

(*b*) Leaves 20—35 cm. long; 3 to 3.8 cm. broad.

Sikkim, at Engo, 3,000′. X. *var.* **spatulata.**

19. Pseudobulbs spherical, about 2.5 cm. in diameter; leaves two, lanceolate, 7—15 cm. long and 18 to 25 mm. broad; peduncle soon curved; raceme longer than peduncle; flowers green; lip broadly ovate.

Tropical valleys below 3,000′; also Assam, Khasia, Nilgiris, Ceylon. XI.
L. viridiflora, Lindley.

— Pseudobulbs ovoid or ovoid-cylindric; flowers ochreous or golden-brownish .. **20**

20. Inflorescence 10 cm. long and less, comparatively few-flowered; flowers ochreous **21**

— Inflorescence 15 to 30 cm. long, many-flowered; flowers golden-brownish; leaves 2—4; lip broadly oblong or ovate, sagittate at the base.

4—6,000′; also Khasia. X—XII.
L. resupinata, Ridley.

21. Pseudobulb bearing 3—5 leaves; peduncle and axis of inflorescence winged; lip quadrate, basal half with 4 swellings.

4—6,000′. IX. **L. platyrrhachis,** Hooker fil.

— Pseudobulbs bearing 2 leaves; peduncle and axis of inflorescence not winged; lip orbicular-oblong, base with short lateral tubercles.

Sittong, 6,000′; also Khasia and Mishmi Hills. VIII, IX. **L. delicatula,** Hooker fil.

DIDICIEA, King and Prain.

— Terrestrial; pseudobulb with a single leaf from its side; leaf stalked, blade ovate, acute, about 38 mm. long and 20 mm. broad; spike lax-flowered, 25—38 mm. long; sepals and petals sub-equal; spur very short.

Lachen valley, probably 12,000′. VII. **D. Cunninghami,** King and Prain.

DENDROBIUM, Swartz.

1. Stems or pseudobulbs growing close together associated into clusters or tufts **2**

— The creeping or pendulous root-stock either bearing at intervals of 7.5 cm. (three or more inches) apart ovoid or oblong-ellipsoid two-leaved pseudo-bulbs or emitting pendulous 60—90 cm. (2 to three feet) long branches bearing at irregular intervals spindle-shaped pseudo-bulbs **33**

2. Pseudobulbs 1.2—5 cm. (one-half to two inches) long; bearing 1 to 3 leaves .. **3**

— Stems (or composite pseudobulbs) longer and usually much longer than 7.5 cm. (3 inches) **5**

3. Flowers 12 mm. and less across .. **4**

— Flowers about 25 mm. (one inch) or more across, in a two- to many-flowered drooping raceme; lip much larger than the sepals and petals, broadly obcordate, changing from primrose to orange with a dark patch near its base; leaf single on the pseudobulb, oblong, notched at the tip, about 2 to 6.5 cm. long.

Foot of hills, common; also from Assam to Perak. III to V.

D. aggregatum, Roxburgh.

4. Pseudobulbs globular, 12—18 mm. in diameter; leaves two, terminal, soon falling off; racemes 2.5 cm. long and less, much shorter than the leaves; flowers white, except the pale-brown lip and its amethyst-coloured mid-lobe.

About 1,000′; also Burma. Cold Season.

D. pygmæum, Lindley.

— Pseudobulbs cylindrical to conical, 12—25 mm. long; leaves 1—3; racemes 5—10-flowered, on a slender stalk; sepals and petals pale green with red nerves; lip brownish-purple, edged pale-green.

5—7,000′; also Khasia. IV, V.

D. porphyrochilum, Lindley.

5. Leaves fleshy, inserted with a broad riding base, oblong or ovate-oblong, rather close-set, less than 5 cm. long; stems erect, straight 6

— Leaves leathery, usually more than 5 cm. in length 7

6. Stems 15 cm. and less high, terete below; leaves less than 2 cm. long; flowers solitary or in pairs, terminal, white or pale pink; lip obtriangular-wedge-shaped with a median yellow line.

Tropical valleys; also Tenasserim. IX, X.
D. terminale, Parish and Reichenbach fil.

— Stems 15—75 cm. high, compressed; leaves 2.5 to 4.5 cm. long; flowers inserted singly at the side of the stem, yellowish-green; lip oblong-wedge-shaped, concave, crisp.

Bottom of tropical valleys; also Bengal, Assam, Burma, Andamans and Nicobars. IV, V. **D. anceps,** Swartz.

7. Flowers densely crowded forming an erect nearly sessile or a stalked nodding head; stems slender-clavate or spindle-shaped 8

— Inflorescence consisting of few-flowered clusters or forming more or less conspicuous racemes 9

8. Head of flowers nearly sessile, about 25 mm. in diameter, yellow marked with red; leaves elliptic-oblong or elliptic lanceolate, 3—7.5 cm. long, concave.

4,000—6,000′, common; also N.-W. Himalaya, Ganjam District and Shan Hills. VIII, IX. **D. bicameratum,** Lindley.

— Head of flowers stalked and nodding, about 50 mm. and more in length and width; sepals and petals dingy-yellow with darker lines; lip orange with a patch of brown nerves on either side of the basal part; leaves broad-elliptic, 10—18 cm. long; side-nerves strong.

Tropical valleys, common; also Assam and Khasia. IV, V. **D. sulcatum,** Lindley.

9. Inflorescence consisting of 2- to 5-flowered terminal, sub-terminal or lateral clusters or of single or of pairs of flowers forming an open or interrupted raceme, total number of flowers on a stem hardly ever exceeding ten, often less **10**

— Inflorescence showy, either composed of numerous racemes or clusters arranged along the stem or of pendulous racemes which may be terminal and consist of many flowers or lateral and drooping .. **20**

10. Flowers in pendulous, nodding or spreading subterminal sometimes also lateral clusters of two to five, usually more than 25 mm. across **11**

— Flowers singly or in pairs inserted at the nodes or forming small lateral clusters or interrupted racemes, mostly 25 mm. and less across **14**

11. Flowers widely open, with a short stumpy spur and spreading sepals and petals, 50—125 mm. across **12**

— Flowers funnel-shaped with a rather slender-conical spur and only moderately spreading sepals and petals, about 25 mm. across **13**

12. Flower-bearing stem leafy, 12—15 mm. thick, coarsely longitudinally ridged; flowers 75—125 mm. across; sepals and petals pure white; lip yellow, broad-obovate, with two tubercled median ridges.

Foot of hills, common; also from Nipal to Burma and the Andamans. V.

D. formosum, Roxburgh.

— Flower-bearing stem leafless, ridged, leafy stem not ridged; flowers 50—75 mm. across, on a peduncle bearing several tubular sheaths; sepals and petals dark-yellow; lip reniform, with a large purple patch near its centre and a pale-yellow margin.

Tendong, 3,000′; also Kumaon, Khasia, Shan Hills. V, VI. **D. clavatum,** Wallich.

13. Stem markedly increasing in thickness from the base towards the middle, here usually more than 6 (often 12) mm. thick, more or less coarsely ribbed, 25—50 cm. long, glabrous; leaves broad-lanceolate, 18—25 mm. broad; petals obovate, like the sepals pale purple; lip spatulate, clawed, white except the yellow base and sometimes a pink patch near the apex.

Tropical valleys up to 3,000′; also from Bhotan to Upper Burma. VI, VII.

D. cumulatum, Lindley

— Stem slightly increasing from the base upwards, less than 6 mm. thick, not ribbed, 15—30 cm. long, covered with short black hairs; leaves narrow-lanceolate, about 6—8 mm. broad; sepals and petals ovate-lanceolate, pure white; lip obtriangular, with two broad side-lobes and a short fringed end-lobe, pale brown veined with orange.

4—8,000′, common; also from Nipal to Khasia. IX—XI. **D. longicornu,** Lindley.

14. Stems upwards 8—11 mm. thick, striated white and green, pendulous, leafless in flower; flowers either single or in twos or threes rising from some of the nodes, widely spreading with long and very slender ovaries; flowers pink or white, the lip broad obovate with a large yellow spot.

Tropical valleys up to 3,500′; also Assam, Khasia, Upper Burma and S. India. IV, V. **D. crepidatum,** Lindley.

— Stems 6 mm. and less thick, slender .. **15**

15. Flowers in clusters of one to four on some of the nodes **16**

— Flowers forming a terminal, rather scanty, often interrupted raceme; flower-bearing stem leafless **18**

16. Flower-bearing stem leafy; flowers golden-yellow, lip marked with purple..

Tropical valleys up to 2,500′. IV—IX. **D. Cathcartii,** Hooker fil.

— Flower-bearing stem leafless .. **17**

17. Stems erect, 15—25 cm. long; flowers white with a patch of dull yellow on the lip; lip not clawed, upper surface covered with gland-tipped hairs.

Tista valley at about 1,200′; also Khasia and Tenasserim. VI. **D. stuposum,** Lindley.

— Stems pendulous, 50—75 cm. long; flowers golden-yellow, sepals and petals edged with purple, end-lobe of lip spotted red.

Tista Valley, at about 2,000′; Engo at about 4,000′.

D. pauciflorum, King and Pantling.

18. Stem erect, 15 to 30 cm. long; sepals and petals pure white, lanceolate; lip oblong-lanceolate, acute, glabrous, white with a yellow spot near the base.

Pamiongtchi and Lachen valley, 6—7,000′; also Khasia. V, VI. **D. candidum,** Wallich.

— Stem pendulous, 30—60 cm. long; sepals and petals pale purple or yellow, ovate, elliptic or rhomboid **19**

19. Flowers 18—22 mm. long, pale purple; lip broad-elliptic, apex abruptly acuminate, upper surface pubescent.

Tropical valleys up to 2,000′; also from Bhotan to Upper Burma. VI—VIII.

D. aduncum, Wallich.

— Flowers 30—38 mm. long, primrose-yellow; lip trapezoidal, with radiating streaks of brown-purple, end-lobe suborbicular, bifid, crisp, middle part of lip with a villous, green crest.

Sittong, 4—5,000′; also Bhotan and Khasia. IV, V. **D. ramosum,** Wallich.

20. Stems terete, cylindrical or attenuated from base to apex or only moderately increasing in thickness upwards, never conspicuously club-shaped, greatest thickness 15 mm. or less **21**

— Stems conspicuously club-shaped, greatest thickness 20—24 mm., flowers in a closely packed, large, sub-terminal raceme .. **32**

21. The erect stems conspicuously attenuated from a thick base upwards, entirely or nearly entirely covered with the sheaths of leaves, 8—25 cm. long; sepals and petals narrow-lanceolate or linear; flowers in spreading or overhanging, thin-stalked, axillary racemes, tinted variously green or greenish-white, 13—18 mm. across .. **22**

—Stems cylindrical or moderately increasing upwards in thickness; sepals oblong or ovate-oblong; petals broadly oblong, elliptic or suborbicular; flowers white, yellow, orange or purple, 18—125 mm. across .. **23**

22. Leaf-blades lanceolate, broadest at the base; sepals lanceolate; petals linear; lip with narrow, pectinate-serrate side-lobes and a shorter, recurved, wavy, acute mid-lobe; flowers of various tints of green, lip slightly spotted with dull purple.

3—6,000′, common; also Khasia. IX, X.
D. eriiflorum, Griffith.

— Leaf-blades narrow-oblong, narrower at the base; sepals linear; petals smaller; lip with narrow laciniate side-lobes, mid-lobe narrow, acute, much recurved, crisp and serrate; flowers pale-green or whitish, lip with a band of radiating red lines along the edges.

3—5,000′, common; also Nipal and Kumaon. IX, X. **D. denudans,** Don.

23. Either the whole stem or at least the separate racemes pendulous **24**

— Stem and inflorescence erect **30**

24. Stem pendulous **25**

— Stem erect, but racemes pendulous or drooping **28**

25. Flowering stem bearing leaves .. **26**

— Flowering stem without leaves .. **27**

26 Stem 150—200 cm. (6—8′) long; internodes about 6 mm. in the middle, nodes 9—12 mm. thick; leaves broad-lanceolate, 7—10 cm. long; flowers 2—4 forming pendulous racemes, golden-yellow; lip orbicular, conspicuously fringed, with or without two oblique dark-purple patches. 4—6,000′; also Assam and Khasia. IX.

D. Hookerianum, Lindley.

— Stem about 13 mm. thick at the middle, thinner towards base and apex, 50—80 cm. long; leaves elongate-lanceolate, 8—17 cm. long; flowers in clusters of 2—4 on the nodes along the upper part of the stem, yellow; lip transversely rounded-oblong, concave, with two brownish-purple, obovate patches and a felty rim along the short-fringed margin.

3—6.000′. common; also from Nipal to Burma. VII—X. **D. chrysanthum,** Wallich.

27. Lip with broad convolute side-lobes, puberulous on both sides; sepals and petals white with violet tips; lip white with a purple spot near the tip, greenish-yellow towards the middle; flowers smelling of violets.

Tropical valleys up to 4,000′, common; also from Garhwal to Bhotan, Sylhet and Burma. VI. **D. amœnum,** Wallich.

— Lip without side-lobes, convolute to form a shell-like tube and pubescent on the upper surface, pale yellow with radiating purple lines; sepals and petals rose or pale-purple.

Tropical valleys up to 3,000′; also Assam to Tenasserim, Bengal and Indian Peninsula. **D. Pierardi,** Roxburgh.

28. Flowers 30—38 mm. across, dull dusky-yellow; racemes arising opposite the base of fallen leaves, lax, 6—14-flowered; stem 60—90 cm. long; leaves broadly ovate-oblong, short-acuminate, 10—15 cm. long, 2.5 to 5 cm. broad; upper surface of lip papillose, with two brownish-purple spots.

2—5,000′; also Assam, Khasia, Burma. VII, VIII. **D. Gibsoni,** Lindley.

— Flowers 50—75 mm. across; racemes inserted near the apex of the stem .. **29**

29. Stem gradually attenuated from base to apex, up to 130 cm. in height; leaves 15—28 mm. broad; flowers brilliant

yellow; lip orbicular, wavy and shortly fringed, with a large round reddish-brown patch.

Tropical valleys up to 4,500′, common, also from Kumaon to Upper Burma. III—V.

D. fimbriatum, *var.* **oculatum,** Hooker.

— Stem thickest in the middle, attenuated towards base and apex; leaves 3—5 cm. broad; flowers ochraceous; sepals with reddish tips and reddish or orange veins; lip forming a globular or pear-shaped pouch, with two large brownish-purple patches inside.

Tropical valleys up to 4,000′; also Kumaon to Tenasserim. V—VII.

D. moschatum, Wallich.

30. Stems either of nearly the same thickness throughout, or slightly thinner upwards, greatest thickness about 6 mm.; flowers 35 to nearly 50 mm. across; petals white, sometimes suffused with pink; lip clawed, with convolute side-lobes and an orbicular mid-lobe with a large purple patch in the middle.

From the foot of the hills to 3,000′; also from Kumaon to Khasia and Chittagong Hills. V.

D. transparens, Wallich.

— Stems increasing in thickness from the base upwards; flowers 50—75 mm. across **31**

31. Lip trowel-shaped, sides of lower part only slightly convolute, disc papillose-pubescent, yellow with radiating red or purple lines; sepals and petals white or pale-ochre coloured.

Tropical valleys up to 3,000′; also from Nipal to Upper Burma, S. India and Ceylon. IV. **D. heterocarpum,** Wallich.

— Lip pubescent, lower part tubular owing to the sides being incurved, end-part ovate, hood-shaped with recurved and spreading edges, centre deep purple, sepals and petals purple except the base.

Up to 5,000′, very common; also Nipal to Upper Burma. IV, V.

D. nobile, Lindley.

32. Internodes of stem distinctly marked off from each other, each narrowest near its base, markedly increasing in thickness upwards, deeply grooved between the coarse rounded ribs; leaves without lateral longitudinal nerves; flowers very closely packed, 35—42 mm. across; sepals and petals pale-yellow, lip orange with paler edges.

Tropical valleys up to 4,000′; also from Nipal to Khasia and Upper Burma. IV, V. **D. densiflorum,** Wallich.

— Internodes of the spindle-shaped stem only indistinctly marked off from each other; ribs on the upper internodes sharp and rather irregular; leaves with fine lateral longitudinal nerves; flowers somewhat laxly packed, 30—35 mm. across;

sepals and petals passing from pale mauve to white, lip deep yellow with a white edge.

1—3,000′; also Nipal to Burma. IV, V.
D. Farmeri, Paxton.

33. Creeping rhizome emitting pendulous, 60—90 cm. long branches bearing at irregular intervals narrowly spindle-shaped pseudobulbs each with one terminal leaf; flowers one or two from the base of the leaf; sepals and petals white; lip oblong-obovate in outline, concave, decurved, side-lobes with erose apices and separated by two fleshy crests, mid-lobe crisp at the lower part, plicate at the edges of the upper broadened part; side-lobes pink, tip of lip pale green.

Tropical valleys, common; also Khasia, Upper Burma, S. India and Ceylon. V.
D. Macraei, Lindley.

— Creeping or pendulous rhizomes bearing directly oblong-ellipsoid or ovoid-oblong, two-leaved pseudobulbs bearing single flowers or few-flowered scapes between the pair of leaves; flowers of various tints of brown 34

34. Flowers 8—9 cm. across; elliptic- or oblong-lanceolate, 10—15 cm. long, 3.8 to 5 cm. broad; sepals and petals greenish-brown with darker brown blotches; lip 3-lobed, middle lobe rhomboid, dark purple with bronze edges.

Sikkim, 4—6,000′; also Nipal, Assam and Khasia. X. **D. amplum,** Lindley.

— Flowers about 3.5 cm. across; leaves 10 cm. and less long **35**

35. Leaves elliptic-oblong, 25 to 30 mm. broad; flowers pale chestnut-brown; lip with rounded lateral lobes and a subreniform middle lobe with a large triangular thickening.

Sikkim, 6—7,000′; also in the Naga Hills. IV. **D. rotundatum,** Bentham.

— Leaves lanceolate, 12 to 18 mm. broad; flowers dull greyish-brown, the lip paler and with a small central patch of yellow.

Sikkim, 5—7,000′; also Khasia and Naga Hills. X. **D. fuscescens,** Griffith.

CIRRHOPETALUM, Lindley.

1. Rhizome naked or the pseudobulbs crowded **2**

— Rhizome covered with fibrous sheaths and emitting many roots, the pseudobulbs inserted on the rhizome either touching or at a distance up to 13 mm. apart, shrivelled, ovoid; leaves narrow-oblong, 10—15 cm. long; flowers 2—5, umbellate; lateral sepal twice as long as the dorals; lip ovate, green; sepals and petals cream-coloured, spotted.

Tendong, 5, 000′; also Nipal to Garhwal. V. **C. maculosum,** Lindley.

2. Pseudobulbs crowded, touching each other **3**

— Distance between the pseudobulbs at least 1 cm., often much more .. 7

3. Pseudobulbs broadly ovoid, about as broad as long; leaves in pairs; flowers in a drooping raceme 4

— Pseudobulbs inverted pear-shaped or slender-conical; leaves single on each pseudobulb 5

4. Leaves oblanceolate-oblong or narrow-oblong, 25—38 mm. broad, falling off after flowering is over: raceme dense, up to 10 cm. long, many-flowered; flowers drooping, about 18 mm. long; sepals dull-yellowish-green changing to brown; dorsal sepal ovate oblong, lateral sepals less than twice as long as the dorsal; petals and oblong lip purplish with white blotches.

5—7,000′. common; also Khasia. X. XI.

C. viridiflorum, Hooker fil.

— Leaves narrow-oblong, 17—20 mm. broad, falling off before flowering time; raceme lax, 4—12-flowered, 3.5—9 cm. long: flowers decurved or spreading, 45—65 mm. long; lateral sepals pale green when young, pale brown when older, about 5—6 times as long as the dorsal; dorsal sepal, petals and lip pale yellow spotted purple and beset with thick purple hairs.

4—6,000′, common also Kumaon to Burma. X. XI.

C. refractum, Zollinger.

5. Pseudobulbs 25—75 mm. long; leaves 7—25 cm. long; flowers spotted purple .. **6**

— Pseudobulbs 8—13 mm. long; leaves 5—10 cm. long; flowers not purple-spotted, pale ochreous; lateral sepals much longer than the dorsal; lip fleshy, ovate-oblong.

4,000′; also Khasia. IV.
C. caespitosum, Wallich.

6. Pseudobulbs inverted pear-shaped, 25—50 cm. long; leaf oblanceolate-oblong, 3.5—4 cm. broad; scape markedly curved; flowers 6—9. pale yellow, spotted purple, lip nearly entirely purple; lateral sepals about twice as long as the dorsal.

2—5,000′. fairly common; also Nipal to Khasia. VII—IX.
C. guttulatum, Hooker fil.

— Pseudobulbs. slender ovoid-conical; 50—75 mm. long; leaf linear-oblong. 2.5—3 cm. broad; scape moderately curved; flowers 10 or more, dirty-yellow, purple-spotted; lateral sepals 3—4 times as long as the dorsal.

5—6,000′. V. **C. elatum,** Hooker fil.

7. Lateral sepals ending in long, thread-like tails **8**

— Lateral sepals not tailed . .. **9**

8. Rhizome about 4 mm. thick; pseudobulbs 25—30 mm. long, ovate-oblong, smooth; leaves elliptic-oblong, 5—10 cm. long; dorsal sepal ovate with a recurved tip, the

tip like those of the narrow-lanceolate petals beset with gland-tipped hairs; lateral sepals with a filiform, 10—18 cm. long tail, the two tails twisted upon each other except at the two ends; petals and sepals yellowish-green, purple-spotted; lip dark-purple; odour of flowers unpleasant.

Warm valleys. X, XI.

C. ornatissimum, Reichenbach fil.

— Rhizome about 2 mm. thick; pseudobulbs 8—13 mm. long, ovoid, furrowed; leaves lanceolate-ovate, 18—25 mm. long; dorsal sepal oblong-ovate; lateral sepals ending each in a filiform, about 3 cm. long tail, the two tails entirely free from each other; sepals and petals white and semi-transparent.

1,500—6,000′. VI, VII.

C. caudatum, King and Pantling.

9. Leaves and inflorescence pendulous .. **10**

— Leaves and scape erect or inclined upwards **11**

10. Leaves 12—24 cm. long, very fleshy; scape 6—12 cm. long; flowers about 18 mm. long; umbel 5—7-flowered; sepals and petals reddish-brown, much mottled; lip purple with deeper blotches.
5,000′. IX.

C. sarcophyllum, King and Pantling, *var.* **maior.**

— Leaves 5—8 cm. long; scape 18—25 mm. long; flowers about 10 mm. long.
3,000′. VI.
C. sarcophyllum, King and Pantling, *var* **minor.**

11\. Pseudobulbs ovoid, ovoid-oblong or inverted pear-shaped . . . 12

— Pseudobulbs ovoid-cylindric, somewhat diminishing in thickness from the rounded base to the apex, copper-coloured, 2.5—4 cm. long and longer, smooth, 4—20 cm. apart; peduncle 3—4 cm. long, bearing a very short, 6—12-flowered raceme; sepals and petals rose-coloured, lip purple.
6—8,000′; also Nipal. IX, X.
C. brevipes, Hooker fil.

12\. Peduncle only a few millimetres long, bearing an umbel of 5—6, dorsally compressed, rose-red darker-spotted flowers; lateral sepals cohering by their inner edges so as to form a single obovate structure; flowers only lasting for a day; whole plant of a coppery hue.
Tropical valleys; also Bhotan and Tenasserim. IV. **C. bhotanense,** Hooker fil.

— Peduncle 3 cm. long and longer . . 13

13\. Flowers drooping, forming a 3—4 flowered cluster; pseudobulbs 1—2 cm. apart; leaves elliptic-oblong, 3—5 cm. long; lateral sepals linear-oblong, acuminate, spreading; lip tapering to an acute apex and having a deep median groove.
7,000—9,000′. VIII. **C. parvulum,** Hooker fil.

— Flowers 5—12 forming a radiating umbel; lateral sepals cohering, at least at first, along their inner edges **14**

14\. Rhizome about 2 mm. thick; pseudobulbs 8—32 mm. in length; leaves 8 cm. and less long **15**

— Rhizome 4—6 mm. thick; pseudobulbs 25—60 mm. in length; leaves 9—23 cm. long **16**

15\. Leaves obovate-oblong, very fleshy, 38—50 mm. long; scape 5—6 cm. long; umbel 10—12-flowered; the coherent sepals ovate-oblong; dorsal sepal greenish with a few brownish-red markings; lateral sepals, petals and lip ochraceous, lip darker.

Foot of hills, common. V.

C. sikkimense, King and Pantling.

— Leaves oblong-lanceolate, 40—80 mm. long; scape 7—10 cm. long, umbel 6—12 flowered; the cohering lateral sepals lanceolate; lateral sepals pale-brown, dorsal sepal and petals deep-violet with darker spot, lip brownish purple.

6—7,000′; also Nipal. VII, VIII.

C. Wallichii, Lindley.

16\. Pseudobulbs 25—32 mm. long, smooth; leaf sessile or nearly so, linear-oblong, 4—8 cm. long; cohering sepals 16—18 mm. long, about half as broad, together obovate-oblong; flowers pink with darker minute spots.

Tista valley, 1,500′. X.

C. Andersoni, Hooker fil.

Pseudobulbs 38—50 mm. long, often irregularly grooved; leaf narrowed into the short grooved petiole, broadly linear, 15—20 cm. long; the cohering lateral sepals about 4 cm. long, lanceolate-linear, together about 4 mm. broad, reddish-brown; lip darker. Odour disagreeable.

Tropical valleys up to 3,000′; also Khasia. V. VI. **C. cornutum,** Lindley.

ANTHOGONIUM, Lindley.

Terrestrial; pseudobulb ovoid-oblong; stem about 10 cm. long; leaves sheathing, linear, plicate, 15—30 cm. long; scape longer than the leaves; racemes 7—15 cm. long, sparsely flowered; flowers forming a right or obtuse angle with the ovary; sepals connate into a narrow tube, free higher up; lip convolute; flowers white or rose-coloured, lip with dark-purple spots.

4—7,000′, common; also Nipal to Burma. VIII, IX **A. gracile,** Lindley.

CHRYSOGLOSSUM, Blume.

Terrestrial, with creeping rhizome; pseudobulbs lanceolate-ovoid, about 7—8 cm. long; leaf very broadly lanceolate, membranous, about 30 cm. long and 10 cm. broad, petiole 10 cm. scape about as long as the leaf; flowers few, forming a lax raceme; sepals and petals green, spotted brown; lip white with a basal yellow spot and marginal reddish spots.

Rishap; also in Bhotan, 3—5,000′. VI. **Ch. erraticum,** Hooker fil.

DIGLYPHOSA, Blume.

Terrestrial, with creeping rhizome; pseudobulbs narrow cylindric, swollen at the base, 15 cm. long; leaf long-petioled, elliptic, plaited, 35—40 cm. long, about half as broad; raceme dense, many-flowered, about 15 cm. long on a stalk twice its length; flowers golden-yellow, smelling unpleasantly; lip clawed, oblong, with two longitudinal minutely hairy lamellæ.

Ched valley, 4,000′. V.

D. macrophylla, King and Pantling

SPATHOGLOTTIS, Blume.

Terrestrial; pseudobulbs globular, 15—18 mm. long, basal part covered with fibres; leaves narrowly lanceolate-linear, 10—20 cm. long; scape lateral, erect, bearing 3—4 flowers forming a lax raceme; flowers pale yellow, 37 mm. vertically, about three-fourth as much horizontally across; lip three-lobed, minutely red-spotted on the lower half.

Lachung valley; also Nipal. VII, VIII.

Sp. ixioides, Lindley.

PACHYSTOMA, Blume.

Terrestrial, with a rather thick rhizome, leafless at flowering time, producing at intervals of about 5 cm. scapes, about 30 cm. high ending in a many-flowered, about 8 cm. long raceme; leaves appearing after flowering time, linear, 4—5-nerved, at least 30 cm. long; flowers greenish-white, often flushed with pink; end-lobe of lip purplish.

Foot of hills; from Garhwal to the Malay Peninsula and the hills of the Peninsula and Ceylon. III. **P. senile,** Reichenbach fil.

TAINIA, Blume.

1. Pseudobulbs narrowly spindle-shaped, about 2.5—4 cm. apart . .. 2

Pseudobulbs ovoid, close together; leaf-blade broad-lanceolate, plaited, 30—45 cm. long, about 8 cm. broad; flowers distant, forming a 25 cm. long raceme terminating a peduncle about twice its length; sepals and petals greenish with brown lines; lip white, the lamellæ yellow spotted pink.

Tropical Valleys up to 2,500′. III.
T. Hookeriana, King and Pantling

2. Leaf-blade 22—30 cm. long, about 6—13 cm. broad, petiole 9—13 cm. long; scape 45—90 cm. long terminated in a lax, many-flowered, 15—24 cm. long raceme; sepals and petals dark-brown; lip yellow.

Tropical valleys up to 2,500′; also Khasia, Sylhet, Cachar and Burma.
T. latifolia, Bentham and Hooker fi

— Leaf-blade 12—15 cm. long, 3—5.5 cm. broad, petiole 5—6 cm. long; scape 78—80 cm. long terminating in a lax, 7—8-flowered raceme; sepals and petals purplish-brown with darker streaks; lip white speckled brown-purple at the lower half, yellow towards the tip.

Mahalderam Peak, 6,000′ and at Chunthang. VII. **T. minor,** Hooker fil.

NEPHELAPHYLLUM, Blume.

1. Stemless, the pseudobulbs arising directly from the creeping rhizome; pseudobulbs closely approximated **2**

— Stem with well-developed internodes arising from the creeping rhizome, the pseudobulbs inserted at the nodes appearing as a short moderate swelling below the leaf-stalk; the heart-shaped leaves 6—10 cm. long, green with a purplish hue and mottled dull-purple; raceme 3—6-flowered; flowers nodding; sepals and petals green, striped purple; lip wedge-shaped, three-lobed, with a knob-like spur, pale-yellow.

Labha, 5,000′; also Khasia. VI.

N. cordifolium, Blume.

2. Pseudobulb gradually passing into the leaf-stalk; leaf-blade 7—9-nerved, 10—13 cm. long, 6—7.5 cm. broad, uniformly green; scape and raceme 20—25 cm. long; raceme rather lax, 6—10-flowered; sepals and petals greenish-brown with dark-brown nerves; lip with large side-lobes and a short triangular end-lobe, white, dotted pink, with a yellow blotch at the base and pink blotch at the tip, spur-less.

Tropical valleys up to 2,500′. III.

N. grandiflorum, Hooker fil.

— Pseudobulb sharply marked off from the petiole; leaf-blade 5—6-nerved. 7.5—10 cm. long; 4.2—6.5 cm. broad, lower surface purple, upper green flushed and mottled with purple. lustre metallic; raceme short, few-flowered; sepals, petals and base of lip red, lip broad-oblong, not lobed, with a broad median band: spur pouch-like, bilobed. entrance closed with long hairs. like the tip of the lip yellow.

Bhotan. 1.500′. VI.

N. pulchrum, Blume. *var.* **sikkimensis,** Hooker fil.

PHAJUS, Lourier.

1. Pseudobulbs large, inverted pear-shaped or stout-conical or stout- and short-cylindric with a rounded base or ovoid, 8—13 cm. long; 5—7 cm. thick .. **2**

— Pseudobulbs none or stem only slightly swollen at its base **4**

2. Scapes rising from the sides of the pseudobulbs; stems 60 cm. or more high; flowers 10—15 cm. across, in a rather open or lax raceme; sepals and petals widely spreading; lip purple (or yellowish), white towards the margin .. **3**

— Scapes arising from the base of the pseudobulb; stems 60 cm. and less high; flowers about 5 cm. across crowded so as to form a dense raceme; flowers yellow; sepals and petals half-erect; end-lobe of lip brown or blotched with brown; spur short-conical.

Tropical valleys; also Nipal and Khasia. IV. **Ph. maculatus,** Lindley.

3. Spur short-conical, not exceeding 6 mm. in length; end-lobe of lip about 2 cm. long; raceme rather dense, the flowers being usually 1.5—2 cm. from each other. Tropical valleys and base of range; also Assam to Indonesia. IV, V.

Ph. Blumei, Lindley.

— Spur narrow-conical, 12—18 mm. in length; end-lobe of lip broad-ovate, about 3 cm. long; raceme rather lax, the flowers being usually 2.5—4 cm. from each other.

Tropical valleys and base of range; also from Assam to the Malay Archipelago and in Ceylon. IV, V.

Ph. Wallichii, Lindley.

4. Raceme arising from the axil of a leaf, decurved, very lax, the distance between the lower flowers being 4—5 cm.; flowers about 3 cm. across; sepals and petals half-erect, like the lip rose-coloured, sometimes white; mid-lobe of lip nearly square; spur very slender-conical, yellow, about 2 cm. long; ovary slender-obconic, up to 4—5 cm. long.

4—6,000′. common; also Assam and Mishmi Hills. IX, X.

Ph. mishmensis, Reichenbach fil.

— Raceme either basal or terminal; flowers 7—9 cm. across 5

5. Scape arising from the base of the 2.5 to 7 cm. long stem; leaves broadly oblong-lanceolate narrowed into a long petiole, 30—40 cm. long, 4—8 cm. broad; raceme 2—3-flowered; petals and sepals widely spreading.

Bhotan Duars. 500′. II.

Ph. nanus, Hooker fil.

— Stem 30—90 cm. high; leaves numerous, lanceolate or lanceolate-linear, 15—30 cm. long and 2.5—5.5 cm. broad, crowded below the terminal, 4—6-flowered nodding raceme; petals and sepals half-erect, pure white; lip either white or yellow with purple or orange veins; upper surface of lip with 7—9 orange ridges. A smaller, epiphytic form occurs below 3,000′.

2—4,000′; also from Garhwal to Burma, and on the Western Ghats. V.

Ph. albus, Lindley.

ACANTHEPHIPPIUM, Blume.

1. Pseudobulbs ovoid, about 13 cm. long and 6 cm. in diameter, with 2—3 transverse annular fine scars; stem from 10—30 cm. high; the terminal leaf 30—40 cm. long and 7—10 cm. broad; sepals and petals dull-white blotched with yellow, sepals purple-tipped, petals spotted purple and yellow; lip with five narrow yellow ridges and a yellow tip.

2—4,000′; also Khasia. IV, V.

A. sylhetense, Lindley.

— Pseudobulbs elongate-inverted pear shaped, 7—10 cm. long; about 3.8 cm. in diameter, clothed upwards with brown sheaths; stems 10—13 cm. high; the terminal leaf 20—30 cm. long and 6.5—13 cm. broad; flowers pale pink with strong red lines, chin and lip tinged yellow.

1,800—3,000′; also Nipal and Khasia. VII, VIII. **A. striatum,** Lindley.

ARUNDINA, Blume.

Stem 120—220 cm. high; leaves narrow-lanceolate, 20—30 cm. long and 18—25 mm. broad; flowers few on the spreading branches of a lax panicle, 7—8 cm. from the tip of the dorsal sepal to the opposite edge of the lobes of the lip; sepals and petals pale pink-purple, lip brilliant rose-purple.

From the base up to 3,000′; also from Nipal to Upper Burma and Nilgiris and Anamalais. IV—IX.

A. bambusifolia, Lindley.

PORPAX, Lindley.

1. Leaves oblanceolate, 30—45 mm. long, present at flowering time, inserted in pairs on the 12 mm. wide, strongly reticulate, disc-shaped pseudobulb; sepals united into a two-beaked pouch, gibbous at the base, sparsely hairy outside edges of lip minutely serrate; flowers uniformly dull-red.

Tropical valleys at the base of the hills. X. **P. fibuliformis,** King and Pantling.

— Leaves broad-lanceolate, about 25 mm. long, not present at flowering time, in pairs on the 8—9 mm. wide, obscurely reticulated, depressed-turbinate pseudobulb; sepals united into a two-lipped hairless tube; edges of lip entire; flowers uniformly dull-brown.

1,500—2,000′; also Tenasserim. X (?)
P. Meirax, King and Pantling.

NOTE.

P. Elwesii, Reichenbach fil., *a species which was probably gathered in British Sikkim, but has not been met with again, differs from P. Meirax only by the lip being somewhat three-lobed and auricled at the base.*

ERIA, Lindley.

1. Inflorescence a dense head of minute flowers 9—13 mm. in diameter; pseudobulbs compressed, slender club-shaped, 7—10 cm. long, bearing at their apex 3—4 lanceolate leaves; flowers white flushed with pink, lateral lobes of lip red.

Tropical valleys; also Khasia and Tenasserim. VIII (?). **E. pumila,** Lindley.

— Flowers single or in clusters or in racemes 2

2. Stems pendulous 3

— Stems creeping or erect 4

3. Leaves lanceolate, 6—10 cm. long, rusty-pubescent; flowers 3—6 in leaf-opposed clusters, 8—9 mm. long, whitish flushed with pink, lip blotched with red at the base.

Tropical valleys up to 2,500′; also Cachar, Khasia, and Tenasserim. V (?).

E. rufinula, Reichenbach fil.

— Leaves linear, blade 16—20 cm. long, 5—12 mm. broad; flowers many in terminal, fascicled racemes, 6—9 mm. across; sepals pale yellowish-green, petals and lip lavender-coloured with brownish blotches.

2—4,000′; also Sylhet, Khasia and Naga Hills. I—IV.

E. paniculata, Lindley.

4. Leaves less than 3.5 cm. long .. **5**

— Leaves more than 3.5 cm. long; usually much longer **6**

5. Pseudobulbs touching, depressed-globular, about 6 mm. broad; leaves oblanceolate, 12—32 mm. long, about 6 mm. broad; scape erect, bearing a small 3—6-flowered raceme; flowers about 6 mm. across, pale-green; lip lanceolate.

Namtse, 4—5,000′; also Nipal, Khasia, Tenasserim. VIII.

E. muscicola, Lindley.

— Stem creeping on trees, much branched, hairy; leaves fleshy, elliptic-ovate or obovate, 8—17 mm. long, 3—9 mm. broad, white-woolly and hairy; flowers solitary, 10—13 mm. long, green flushed with yellow, base of lip with a brownish-purple patch.

Tropical valleys up to 3,000′; also Khasia and Pegu. V, VI.

E. dasyphylla, Parish and Reichenbach fil.

6. Leaves flat **7**

— Leaves slender-cylindric, 7—18 cm. long, fleshy, 1—4 on very short stems rising at intervals of 5 and more cm. from a woolly, about 3 mm. thick rhizome; flowers 1—4 on a 2.5—5 cm. long peduncle, about 13 mm. long; sepals and petals covered with white wool outside, inner surface golden-brown; lip dark-brown.

Tropical valleys and base of range; also Tenasserim and Malay Peninsula. V.

E. pannea, Lindley.

7. Pseudobulb either assuming the form of a stem or lengthening into a stem, the whole slender-cylindric or narrow-club-shaped **8**

— Pseudobulbs clearly developed as such, stout cylindric, ovoid-slender-conical, or shortly ovoid or ellipsoidal, never stem-like **13**

8. Pseudobulbs slender-club- or spindle-shaped **9**

— Stems slender-cylindrical, either of nearly the same thickness throughout or gradually attenuated upwards **10**

9. Pseudobulbs deeply furrowed, 10—15 cm. long, 1—2 cm. at the thickest part; leaves 7—14 cm. long, 1.5—2 cm. broad; racemes from the axils of sheaths, 5—8 cm. long, 6—9-flowered; flowers about 10 mm. across; sepals and petals dull-yellow with red-brown nerves; end-lobe of lip bright-yellow, edged brown.

Tista valley, 1,500′. IV.

E. confusa, Hooker fil.

— Pseudobulbs not grooved, 6—10 cm. long, 5—9 mm. at the thickest part; leaves 5—8 cm. long, 1.2—1.7 cm. broad; flowers one or two on short stalks, 6—7 mm. across, pale-yellow.

Tropical valleys; also Mergui. IX (?).

E. biflora, Griffith.

10. Leaves two, terminal; sheaths only at the base; raceme single **11**

— Leaves three or more, inserted higher up on the stem; sheaths all along the flowering stem; racemes several **12**

11. Sheath tubular; leaves 12—15 cm. long, 3—4 cm. broad; raceme spreading, bearing 4—6 flowers; flowers nearly 2 cm. across, sweet-scented; sepals and petals white (or purplish); lip flushed with purple outside, side-lobes with purple streaks, end-lobe yellow.

5—6,000′; also Khasia. XI, XII.

E. coronaria, Reichenbach fil.

— Sheaths lanceolate, short, fibrous; leaves 6—10 cm. long, 1.2—2.3 cm. broad; spike erect and strict, one-sided, bearing many flowers; flowers about 3 mm. across, white flushed with pink, sides of lip streaked yellow. —

1,000—4,000′, common; also Nipal, Assam, Naga, Khasia. XI—II.

E. stricta, Lindley.

12. Stem 60—90 cm. high, enveloped in grooved tubular sheaths; leaves six or more on the upper part of the stem, 2.5—4 cm. broad; flowers in a lax raceme, pale-brown with darker lines, lip with three pale-green ridges.

Rissisom, 6,000′; also Khasia and Ganjam. X—XII. **E. bambusifolia,** Lindley.

— Stem 10—15 cm. high, when young with several tubular sheaths; leaves 3—6 (sometimes 2), crowded at the end of the stem, 9—19 mm. broad; flowers in rather dense racemes; sepals and petals pure white; ridges on lip and its mid-lobe yellowish, side-lobes red.

5—7,000′, fairly common. VII, VIII.

E. graminifolia, Lindley.

13. Pseudobulbs crowded or in close-set rows **14**

— Distance between pseudobulbs 2—9 cm. **18**

14. Flowers in open racemes or in terminal clusters **15**

— **Flowers very many, small, in dense decurved spikes; pseudobulbs stout-cylindric, when young covered with large loose sheaths; leaves 4—6, broadly oblanceolate, 10—18 cm. long; spikes several; flowers subglobose, about 6 mm. in diameter, white or pale straw-coloured, lip tinged yellow.**

2—6,000′, common; also Garhwal to Tenasserim. VII, VIII.

E. convallarioides, Lindley.

15. Pseudobulbs ovoid or ellipsoidal, 4—8 cm. long, 2.5—3 cm. thick; bearing a single leaf with a broad-lanceolate, 17—30 cm. long, 3.5—8.5 cm. broad blade narrowing into a long, channelled petiole; inflorescence a 3-flowered raceme; peduncle rising from an undeveloped pseudobulb and sheathed by large bracts; flowers drooping, about 25 mm. from base to tip of the yellowish-green sepals; petals yellowish, lip pale-purplish; the flowers smelling of tincture of opium.

500—3,000′; also Nipal and Khasia. X—I.

E. carinata, Gibson.

— Pseudobulbs narrow-conical or subcylindric, always narrowing upwards, 3.5—10 cm. long, 1—2 cm. thick; leaves sessile or very shortly petioled; flowers less than 15 mm. across **16**

16. Pseudobulb slender conical of one piece, 5—10 cm. long, 1.8—2 cm. thick near the ovoid base; leaves 12—15 cm. long, 2.5—

3.5 cm. broad; flowers in 3 or more spreading, lax, racemes, about 18 mm. across, pale-yellow; lip with 3 red lamellæ running lengthways.

1—3,000′; also from Chittagong to Singapore. IV. **E. bractescens,** Lindley.

— Pseudobulbs stout-spindle-shaped (consisting of 3—4 links), less than 5 cm. long and less than 1.5 cm. thick (when young closed with sheaths and then imitating a short, cylindrical stem), leaves usually less than 2.5 cm. broad; flowers white or dirty-white **17**

17. Flowers 2—4 forming a terminal cluster on the 1—3, about 5—7 cm. long and about 2 mm. thick peduncles; ovary and pedicel together 15—20 mm. long and about 1 mm. thick; flowers about 22 mm. long; sepals half-upright; end-lobe of lip tinged with yellow.

1,500—2,000′; also Khasia. VI, VII. **E. acervata,** Lindley

— Flowers 6—8 forming a lax raceme at the upper end of the solitary, 5—7 cm. long and 2 mm. thick peduncle; ovary and pedicel 8 mm. long and about 2 mm. thick; flowers 7 mm. and less long; sepals erect; end-lobe of lip yellow with some red markings.

6—9,000′; also Khasia. VI. **E. excavata,** Lindley.

18. Pseudobulbs 2.5 cm. and less from each other; raceme decurved or drooping, 15—25-flowered; flowers very fragrant .. **19**

— Pseudobulbs 4—8 cm. from each other; raceme straight or slightly bent, erect or nearly so, about 10—12-flowered .. 20

19. Pseudobulbs slender-conical, nearly cylindrical, 7—10 cm. long, about 2 cm. thick below, narrowing upwards to 1 cm.; leaves 15—20 cm. long; raceme drooping; flowers crowded, pale green, parts striped purplish-brown.

5—6,000′; also Manipur. III, IV.

E. vittata, Lindley.

— Pseudobulbs ovoid-oblong, about 2.5—3 cm. thick near the base, 2 cm. at the upper end, 5—7 cm. long; leaves 20—30 cm. long; raceme decurved, rather lax; flowers white with some red spots on the side-lobes of the lip.

Bottom of hot valleys; also Tenasserim. VII, VIII.

E. fragrans, Reichenbach fil.

20. Rhizome 8 mm. thick and thicker, clothed with tubular sheaths; sheath of sub-cylindric, 7—10 cm. long pseudobulbs conspicuously furrowed; leaves 15—23 cm. long, 18—38 mm. broad; raceme from the base of the pseudobulb, felty, straight, 25—30 cm. long; sepals and petals spreading and green; lower half of lip purple.

Warm valleys and base of range; also Kumaon to Bhotan. IV.

E. flava, Lindley.

— Rhizome 2—3 mm. thick, smooth; pseudobulbs ovoid clothed at the base with the fibrous remains of sheaths; leaves 10—15 cm. long; 20—25 mm. broad; racemes 1 or 2, from the top of the pseudobulb, straight or slightly curved, 10—12 cm. long; flowers remaining more or less closed, pale-green with some brown streaks on the lip.

3,000—5,000′, fairly common. II, III.

E. clausa, King and Pantling.

TYLOSTYLIS, Blume.

Stems built up of 4—6 pseudobulbs in series, the lowest about 10 cm. long, the upper ones rapidly diminishing in length; leaves arising at the junctions, leathery, sessile, broad-lanceolate, 12—20 cm. long; racemes from outside the leaves and shorter than they; flowers few, small, ochre-yellow, outside dull-white; lip with a purplish-brown, basal patch.

500—3,500′; also Khasia. II.

T. discolor, Hooker fil.

CŒLOGYNE, Lindley.

1. Inflorescence rising from the top of the pseudobulb **2**

   Inflorescence rising from the base of the pseudobulb **6**

2. Pseudobulbs slender conical or spindle-shaped, 4—6 times as long as thick .. **3**

— Pseudobulbs oblong ovoid, about twice as long as thick 4

3. Pseudobulbs 10—13 mm. thick; leaves stalked, elliptic-lanceolate; flowers 18—25 mm. across, 4—8 arranged in a raceme on a slender petiole clothed below the flowers with numerous small imbricate bracts and bent zigzag; end-lobe of lip subquadrate; flowers pale-green flushed with yellow, lip with reddish markings.

6—7,000′; also Naga and Khasia Hills. V, VI.

C. longipes, Lindley.

— Pseudobulbs 20—26 mm. thick; leaves sessile, elliptic-oblong; flowers 5—6 cm. across, three, expanding one after the other, pale-brown, lip with blackish-brown markings and hairs; end-lobe of lip broad-oblong.

2—6,000′; also from Nipal to Khasia. X—XII.

C. ovalis, Lindley.

4. Flowers 35—40 mm. across; 10 and more forming a somewhat two-rowed raceme; leaves 18—35 cm. long; sepals and petals white with an ochre-yellow tint, lamellæ of lip with a spot of yellow and pink, lower parts of them yellow.

4—6,000′; also Garhwal to Upper Burma. V, VI. **C. elata,** Lindley.

— Flowers 12—20 mm. across. less than 10 in a raceme; length of leaves not exceeding 18 cm. 5

5. Leaves elliptic-oblong, 3—5 cm. long; flowers about 20 mm. across; petals thread-like; end-lobe of lip subquadrate, orange-brown, with undulate margin and two converging lamellæ; sepals and petals yellow-brown.

Lachen valley, 6—7,000′; also Nipal and Khasia. VI. **C. prolifera,** Lindley.

— Leaves broad-lanceolate, 10—18 cm. long; flowers 12 mm. across; petals linear; end-lobe of lip obcordate-wedge-shaped; flowers pale-yellow.

Up to 5,000′, very common; also Naga and Khasia Hills. V—VII.
C. flavida, Wallich.

6. Flowers solitary, or more rarely two, on a short peduncle not longer than the pseudobulb **7**

— Flowers three to many, or if two only, then the peduncle much longer than the pseudobulb **11**

7. Basal part of end-lobe of lip oblong with parallel wavy edges with two longitudinal lamellæ, the terminal part ovate, brown, with two dark-brown spots; sepals and petals white; leaves narrow-lanceolate; plants often occurring in large masses.

500—4,000′; also Nipal, Khasia, Tenasserim. IV, V. **C. uniflora,** Lindley.

— End-lobe of lip not separated into a basal and apical part or the whole lip not clearly differentiated into side- and end-lobes .. **8**

8. Pseudobulbs ovoid or ovoid-oblong, less than 2 cm. in diameter; leaves 5—10 cm. long 9

— Pseudobulbs top-shaped (turbinate), rather abruptly passing into a short, conical tip (umbonate), 2.5—4 cm. in diameter; leaves 10—20 cm. long .. **10**

9. Pseudobulbs ovoid or ellipsoidal, less than 2.5 cm. long; lip subreniform when flattened out, cordate at the base, narrowed to the retuse apex, wih five to seven thin parallel longitudinal ridges and reddish mottlings; sepals and petals white flushed with violet.

7—11,000′; also Kumaon. V, VI.

C. Hookeriana, Lindley.

— Pseudobulbs ovoid-oblong, 3—4 cm. long; lip, when flattened out, broad-elliptic, nearly orbicular with emarginate apex and sharply denticulate margin, upper surface with 7—9 fringed lamellæ; sepals and petals white, central part of lip yellow with brown spots, marginal parts purple-speckled.

7—8,500′; also Nipal. II, III.

C. humilis, Lindley.

Pseudobulbs less than 2.5 cm. in diameter, enclosed in a dense network of fibres; flowers 5—7.5 cm. across; sepals and petals white, sometimes with pink lines; lip sub-elliptic in outline with narrow side-lobes, a broad end-lobe with purple and yellow markings; leaves broadly oblanceolate, 10—20 cm. long, absent at flowering time.

1,600—3,000′; also Nipal to Khasia. X, XI. **C. maculata,** Lindley.

— Pseudobulbs 2.5—4 cm. in diameter, sparsely sheathed by loose fibres; flowers 7.5—10 cm. across, rose-coloured; lip, when flattened out, trapezoid in outline, with dentate edges, the central part with 5 dentate lamellæ; sometimes the whole flower white.

6—8,000′; very common; also from Garhwal to Burma (?). **C. præcox,** Lindley.

11. Inflorescence of two to four flowers, corymbose; mid-lobe of lip acuminate .. **12**

— Inflorescence of six and more flowers, racemose; mid-lobe of lip obtuse; rounded or truncate **13**

12. Pseudobulbs ellipsoid or bipyramidal, about 15 mm. thick, inserted on a 3—7 mm. thick rhizome; leaves shortly stalked, lanceolate, about 6—9 cm. long; flowers 2—3, inodorous, white except some yellow streaks and a yellow blotch on the lip.

6—7,500′. VII. **C. occultata,** Hooker fil.

— Pseudobulbs ovoid or obovoid, 17—20 mm. thick, on an 8—10 mm. thick rhizome; leaves narrowed to a sessile base, lanceolate, 10—18 cm. long; flowers 3—4, sweet-scented; sepals and petals pure-white; basal part of lip brown, middle part with 4 yellow blotches, end-part white.

6—8,500′, common; also Bhotan and Khasia. IV, V. **C. corymbosa,** Lindley.

13. Raceme drooping or pendulous .. **14**

— Raceme erect; pseudobulbs cylindric, somewhat thicker near the base, 7—10 cm. long, furrowed; leaves oblanceolate narrowed into a channelled petiole, 15—20 cm. long; sepals and petals white; lateral lobes of lip with two yellow, red-margined blotches, end-lobe broadly ovate, constricted and with two spots at the base.

4—7,000′, common; also Kumaon to Assam. V, VI.

C. ochracea, Lindley.

14. Leaves linear-oblong or linear-lanceolate, 18—32 mm. broad; pseudobulbs ovoid-oblong **15**

— Leaves elliptic, 5—10 cm. broad; pseudobulbs cylindric; flowers about 5 cm. across; pale-brown; basal part squarish oblong, with three darker ridges and broad side-lobes; end-lobe ovate with wavy borders.

3—5,000′; also Nipal to Burma. X—XII.

C. fuscescens, Lindley.

15. Raceme pendulous, about 6-flowered; flowers pure white except the yellow lamellæ on the lip, 6—9 cm. across; lower part of lip with two large side-lobes with four-fimbriate lamellæ between, end-lobe squarish with two prominent lamellæ.

5—8,000′, common; also Kumaon to Khasia. III, IV.

C. cristata, Lindley.

— Raceme decurved, about 9—10-flowered, lax, axis very slender; flowers on the whole brown, less than 5 cm. across; lip with two large side-lobes, three ridges and an oblong, reflexed end-lobe; flowers smelling disagreeably.

3,000—5,500′, common; also from Nipal to Burma. III—V. **C. flaccida,** Lindley.

PANISEA, Lindley.

Pseudobulbs crowded, ovoid or ovoid-oblong, translucent, 15—25 mm. long, 2-leaved; leaves lanceolate, 5—8 cm. long; raceme pendulous, on a thread-like peduncle, about as long as the leaves; flowers about 13 mm. across; sepals keeled, like the petals and lip white, streaked brown.

6,000′; also Nipal and Khasia. IX, X. **P. parviflora,** Lindley.

OTOCHILUS, Lindley.

1. Leaves elliptic-oblong, more than 13 mm. broad, conspicuously plaited; axis of raceme manifestly zigzaged, not lengthening after flowering **2**

— Leaves linear-lanceolate, 10—12 mm. broad, scarcely plaited; axis of raceme nearly or entirely straight, much lengthening after flowering; lower flowers about 5 mm. from each other; flowers about 15 mm. from tip of dorsal sepal to tip of lip;

lip broadly linear, about by 1|5 to 1|6 shorter than the lateral sepals; floral axis, base of lip, ovary and fruit brown; sepals and petals white.

3—6,000′, common; also from Nipal to Manipur. XII. **O. fusca,** Lindley.

2. Leaves 35—70 mm. broad; distance between flowers about 13 mm.; flowers about 30 mm. across, mainly white, but a patch on the sac of the lip, the column and the floral axis brown.

4—6,000′, abundant; also from Nipal to Burma. X—I. **O. porrecta,** Lindley.

— Leaves 13—25 mm. broad; distance between flowers 5 mm. and less; flowers 15—17 mm. across, white.

3—5,000′, common; also Nipal to Khasia. VI. **O. alba,** Lindley.

PHOLIDOTA, Lindley.

1. Pseudobulbs tufted, bearing a single leaf, slender-conical with an ovoid base, furrowed; leaf 15—30 cm. long, broadly elliptic-lanceolate, narrowing to a 3 cm. long petiole; raceme drooping, densely and many-flowered, 20—25 cm. long; flowers about 7 mm. across; lip with two hatchet-shaped side-lobes, a rectangular middle part and two end-lobules separated by a broad bay; flowers pale-brown.

Foot of hills to 5,000′, common; also Kumaon to Malay Peninsula, Deccan and Ceylon and Andamans. V—VIII. **Ph. imbricata,** Lindley.

— Pseudobulbs at some distance from each other or the internodes of the stem like pseudobulbs; leaves two on the pseudobulbs or on the pseudobulb-like links of the stem 2

2. Raceme 15—25 cm. long, drooping, the flowers arranged in two rows at a distance of about 5 mm. from each other, about 8—10 mm. across; the sepals and petals pale yellowish-green, the lip and column pinkish-brown; rhizome thick, fleshy, short, bearing spindle-shaped pseudobulbs.

3—6,000′; also Khasia. XI, XII.

Ph. rubra, Lindley.

— Raceme less than 13 cm. long .. 3

3. Stem not jointed, slender, 30—60 cm. long, giving off at intervals spindle-shaped, translucent pseudobulbs and several short, few-flowered racemes; flowers 5—7 mm. across; sepals connivent, like the petals green, the end-lobe of the lip with four yellow patches.

5—7,000′; also Naga and Khasia Hills. X—XII. **Ph. protracta,** Hooker fil.

— Stem built up of cylindrical pseudobulb-like links 4

4. The bracts falling off when the flowers expand, rhombic; flowers approximately in two opposite rows, whitish or pale green .. 5

— Bracts persistent, on one side of the raceme, imbricating, truncate, the flowers covering the opposite side of the raceme, 3—4 mm. long.

2—4,000′; also from Nipal to Bhotan. VIII, IX. **Ph. recurva,** Lindley.

5. Flowers 8—10 mm. across, white tinged with brownish-pink.

From the foot of the hills to 4,000′, common; also Kumaon to Upper Burma. VI, VII, VIII. **Ph. articulata,** Lindley, *var.* **genuina.**

— Flowers 5 mm. across; sepals green, petals pale-green, lip brown.

2—4,000′; also Khasia. VII, VIII. **Ph. articulata, Lindley,** *var.* **Griffithii,** King and Pantling.

TIPULARIA, Nuttall.

Leaf solitary, broad-ovate, 7—13 cm. long, plaited, 7-nerved; raceme from the base of the pseudobulb, erect; flowers about 8 mm. long.

10—12,000′. VIII. **T. Josephi,** Reichenbach fil.

MONOMERIA, Lindley.

Rhizome woody; pseudobulbs 5—8 cm. apart, ovoid or ellipsoidal; leaf solitary, oblong, 16—30 cm. long, 2.5—3 cm. broad; scape from the base of the pseudobulb; raceme lax; flowers yellow with bold brown markings.

Tropical valleys; also Nipal and Khasia. II. **M. barbata,** Lindley.

ACROCHÆNE Lindley.

Pseudobulbs ovoid, about 2.5 cm. apart; leaf solitary, linear oblong, 15—24 cm. long, about 3.5 cm. broad; scape from the base of the pseudobulb, raceme lax, many-flowered; flowers pale yellowish-green with purple-brown dots and streaks.

5—6,000′. X, XI. .. **A. punctata,** Lindley.

AGROSTOPHYLLUM, Blume.

1\. Heads of flowers less than 20 mm. in diameter; stems covered with sheaths all along or for the greater part of their length, increasing in thickness from the base upwards **2**

— Heads of flowers 30—38 mm. in diameter; stems nearly of the same thickness throughout, base of sheaths for the greater part of their length 2—5 cm. apart **3**

2\. Stems tufted, reaching a thickness of nearly 2 cm. (incl. sheaths); lip saccate at the base; flowers white with pale yellow patches on the mid-lobe of the lip.

Tropical valleys; also Khasia. VIII. **A. khasianum,** Griffith.

— Stems rising from the rhizome at distances of about 2.5 cm. from each other, greatest thickness, including sheaths, less than 1 cm.; flowers white except the dark crimson column and anther.

About 2,000′. VI, VII.

A. brevipes, King and Pantling.

3. Leaves narrow-lanceolate, broadest about 3 cm. from their base, 6—9 times as long as broad; mid-lobe of lip broad-ovate; flowers exceedingly numerous, about 3 mm. wide, yellowish.

Tista valley, 1,200′. VIII.

A. myrianthum, King and Pantling.

— Leaves lanceolate-linear, broadest 1—2 cm. from the base, 10—12 times as long as broad; mid-lobe of lip reniform in outline, bilobulate; flowers numerous, about 6 mm. long, reddish.

6,000′, common. VI, VII.

A. callosum, Reichenbach fil.

RITAIA, King and Pantling.

Stem much branched; leaves fleshy, lanceolate, subterminal and single at the end of the branches; flowers singly or in pairs on a short, terminal peduncle, about 6 mm. long, pale-yellow.

Tendong, 5,000′. V, VI.

R. himalaica, King and Pantling.

IONE, Lindley.

1. Pseudobulbs 8—13 mm. long; scape 1—2-flowered **2**

— Pseudobulbs 13—35 mm. long; scape ending in a 6- to many-flowered raceme .. **3**

2. Flowers about 9 mm. across, sepals and petals yellowish, lip purple.

Bhotan, Baxa; 6,000′. IV.

I. Andersoni, King and Pantling.

— Flowers about 12 mm. across, pale-green. Tendong, 6,000′.

I. intermedia, King and Pantling.

3. Rhizome 1—2 mm. thick; leaves 7—9 cm. long; scape together with the raceme 7—9 cm. long; flowers 6—8, about 10 mm. long; sepals and petals pale and translucent with claret-coloured nerves; lip claret-coloured.

6—7,000′, very common; also Nipal to Khasia. X—XI. **I. bicolor,** Lindley.

— Rhizome about 5 mm. thick; scape together with the raceme more than 25 cm. long; leaves 12—20 cm. in length **4**

4. Raceme deflexed terminating the erect scape; flowers 15—20 or more, about 8 mm. long, greenish flushed with dull purple; sepals unequal; lip shorter than the lateral sepals, fleshy, ovate-oblong.

3,600—4,000′; also from Nipal to Tenasserim. IV, V.
I. scariosa, King and Pantling.

— Scape and raceme straight and erect; flowers 10 or less, 22—27 mm. long, sepals nearly equal, oblong-lanceolate, like the smaller petals transparent with pink reticulations; lip nearly as long as the sepals, dark-purple, oblong-lanceolate.

6,000′, very common; also Bhotan. X, XI.
I. brevipes, King and Pantling.

CRYPTOCHILUS, Wallich.

1. Pseudobulbs oblong-ellipsoidal or ovoid; flowers 20—25 mm. long, spreading; sepaline tube ovoid-cylindric, scarlet, ending in triangular, dirty-white to dark-purple tips; petals, lip and column bright-yellow.

5—7,000′, common; also Nipal to Khasia. VI—VIII. **C. sanguinea,** Wallich.

— Pseudobulbs cylindric; flowers about 6 mm. long, nodding, yellow; sepaline tube ovoid, urn-shaped.

5—7,000′; also Bhotan and Naga Hills. V, VI. **C. lutea,** Wallich.

CALANTHE, Lindley.

1. Inflorescence, rising directly from the jointed, spindle-shaped rhizome, resembling a closely packed basket of flowers on

a 10—30 cm. long scape; leaves 60—90 cm. long, 7—13 cm. broad; flowers yellow, 20 mm. long; lower part of lip with two side-lobes and two prominent lamellæ, end-lobe squarish, emarginate.

Bhotan. Naru valley, 3,000′; also Khasia. X. **C. densiflora,** Lindley.

— Inflorescence on the same stem as the leaves, forming an elongated or contracted raceme; flowers never entirely yellow .. 2

2. Spur absent or less than half as long as the ovary and then short-conical, straight 3

— Spur longer than half the ovary, cylindrical, often curved 8

3. Spur entirely absent 4

— Spur short-conical, 2—4 mm. long .. 6

4. Inflorescences one to three arising from the nodes near the middle or below the middle of the slender stem, overtopped by the leafy upper part of the stem; base of stem only little thicker; petals and sepals pure white, lip white with a yellow band along the middle and a transverse band at the base of the end-lobe.

Rangbi, 6,000′. X. **C. gracilis,** Lindley.

Inflorescences rising from or near the top of the short stem, overtopping the leaves; pseudobulbs broadly ovoid 5

5. Leaves 2—3, broadly oblanceolate, 20—38 cm. long, 5—8 cm. broad; lower flowers of the lax raceme 3—4 cm. from each other; sepals and petals green outside and white-edged, yellowish-green inside; lip with a purple fleshy ridge.

Lachen valley, 6,000′; also westwards to Kashmir. **C. tricarinata,** Lindley.

— Leaves 5—7, oblong, acuminate, 10—15 cm. long, 4—5 cm. broad; lower flowers of the rather dense raceme less than 2 cm. from each other; flowers pale-lavender.

6—7,000′; also from Simla to Khasia. VII, VIII. **C. puberula,** Lindley.

6. Flowers about 8 mm. long, dull-brown, soon deflexed; sepals and petals connivent; lip with three tubercled ridges, end-lobe broader than long, entire.

Rangbi, 6,000′; Lachen valley, 7,000′; also Khasia. **C. Mannii,** Hooker fil.

— Flowers 25—39 mm. across, half-erect or widely spreading, never deflexed; sepals and petals spreading . . . 7

7. Stem built up of 5—6 cylindrical links, 15—20 cm. long, bearing several unequal leaves near the top; peduncles 1—2, from the axils of the lowest leaves, together with the raceme 45—75 cm. long, beset below the flowers with numerous, horizontally spreading lanceolate bracts; sepals and petals ochre-yellow mottled purplish-

brown; lip longer than the sepals, narrowly clawed, end-lobe deeply bilobed.

Shady places, 3,500′—7,000′; also E Nipal. IX, X. **C. biloba,** Lindley.

— Stem 10 cm. and less long; peduncle nude; end-lobe of lip entire or emarginate, not two-lobed **8**

8. Pseudobulbs about 12 mm. long oblong-ovoid; leaves narrow-lanceolate, 2 cm. and less broad; flowers from tip of dorsal sepal to tip of lip less than 2 cm. across; lip truncate-obovate, long-clawed, acuminate, with two lamellæ, white with a pink basal mark; sepals and petals brown with green lines.

Mahalderam Peak, 6,000′. VII.
C. trulliformis, King and Pantling.

— Pseudobulbs about 25 mm. long, ovoid; leaves oblong, 6—9 cm. broad; flowers 3—4 cm. from tip of dorsal sepal to tip of lip; lip truncate-obovate, long-clawed emarginate, with three fleshy lamellæ; flowers dull-purple or brick-red with white lines, outside flushed with white.

6—9,000′; also from Kumaon to Bhotan. V, VI. **C. brevicornu,** Lindley.

9. Length of raceme 10 cm. and less .. **10**

— Raceme at least 15 cm. long, often much longer **11**

10. Pseudobulbs ovoid subcylindric, 2—2.5 cm. long, greatest thickness 1 cm. with 2—3 transverse rings; larger leaves broadly oblanceolate, blade 15—20 cm. long; inflorescence overtopping the leaves; flowers 4—5, rather distant, 10—15 cm. across; sepals and petals white tipped green; lip, when flattened out, semicircular, edge incisedly fringed, dull red, its base and the cylindric spur pale yellow.

Lachen valley, 6—10,000′. VII, VIII.

C. alpina, Hooker fil.

— Pseudobulbs narrowly cylindric, 3—5 cm. long, greatest thickness less than 1 cm. with about 2 transverse rings near the base; leaves long-petioled, blade elliptic, 12—18 cm. long, 6—8 cm. broad; raceme corymbose, 2.5—5 cm. long; flowers 20 mm. across; flowers crowded, inflorescence not longer than the leaves; sepals and petals white, sepals tipped green outside; lip with oblanceolate side-lobes and an obovate, bilobulate end-lobe, lip with a violet blotch near its base and a yellow callosity; spur contracted at base and apex.

Terai and valleys up to 2,000′; also Garhwal and Khasia. V, VI.

C. alismifolia, Lindley.

11. Leaves lanceolate-linear, 60—90 cm. long, less than 4 cm. broad; scape with the dense-flowered raceme 60—120 cm. long; flowers 25 mm. and less across, sweet-scented, sepals and petals yellowish-green,

lip without lateral lobes, quadrate, bilobulate, bright-yellow; spur slender club-shaped.

Chungthang, 6,000′. V.
C. Whiteana, King and Pantling.

— Leaves elliptic or elliptic-lanceolate, 15—35 cm. long, at least 5 cm. broad; lip with side-lobes **12**

12. Side-lobes of lip divergent, forming an angle of about 60° with the middle line of the lip; raceme rather lax; sepals and petals green or yellowish-green .. **13**

— Side-lobes of lip directed forwards, forming an angle of about 30° with the middle line of the lip; raceme dense; sepals and petals white or violet **14**

13. Pseudobulbs ovoid, about 2.5 cm. long; distance between tip of dorsal sepal and tip of lip about 25 mm.; spur stout-cylindric, slightly club-shaped, about as long as the sepals, but considerably shorter than the ovary; side-lobes of lip linear-oblong, mid-lobe deeply cleft into two subcircular lobules, white with an elongated patch of yellow along the middle.

6—8,000′. IV, V. **C. chloroleuca,** Lindley.

— Pseudobulbs shortly-spindle-shaped, 18—30 mm. long, ringed: distance between tip of dorsal sepal and tip of lip 32—40 mm.; spur slender-cylindrical. curved, nearly as long as the stalked ovary; side-lobes of lip elliptic-oblong, mid-lobe divided into two spreading oblong lobules; lip pure-white with a yellow swelling.

4—6,000′; at Rangbi 6,000′. VI.
C. herbacea, Lindley.

14. Pseudobulbs ovoid, about 12 mm. long, with finely marked annular scars; flowers about 25 mm. across, pure-white, not crowded, sweet-scented; lip longer than the sepals; side-lobes falcate, acute; end-lobe deeply divided into two truncately obovate lobules.

East of Jaldacca river, 800′; also Khasia and Manipur. IV. **C. angusta,** Lindley.

Pseudobulbs conical, with strongly marked annular scars, 5—8 cm. long; flowers about 5 cm. across, in a crowded, depressed raceme, violet, lip as long as the sepals; side-lobes oblong, tip rounded; end-lobe pentagonal in outline, emarginate; swellings yellow.

1,500—4,000′, common; also Nipal and Deccan. VIII, IX. **C. Masuca,** Lindley.

YOANIA, Maximowicz.

Rhizome densely clothed with small scales; stem erect, 5—10 cm. high; bearing a few fleshy bracts; flowers white, about 25 mm. long; lip slipper-shaped, not spurred.

Chungthang, 6,000′; also Naga Hills.
Y. Prainii, King and Pantling.

EULOPHIA, R. Brown.

1. Tuber inverted pear-shaped or spherical; flowers scattered **2**

— Tuber more or less irregularly oblong, horizontal, or oblique, flowers usually forming a well-defined raceme **3**

2. Inflorescence branched; pseudobulb pear-shaped, 2.5—10 cm. long; stem slender-cylindric, sometimes 90 cm. long, rising from the side of the pseudobulb; flowers about 18 mm. across; sepals and petals green with reddish nerves; lip obovate, white side-lobes narrow, end-lobe nearly circular, upper surface with five red ridges.

Foot of hills; also extending to Ceylon and Singapore. III. **E. graminea,** Lindley.

— Inflorescence unbranched; tuber spherical, 5—7 cm. in diameter; flowers about seven; sepals nearly erect, pale-green with brown markings outside; petals pale-green; lip oblong, deflexed, margin wavy, pale-green at the base, white in the middle, flushed pink at the tip.

Tropical valleys, up to 1,500′; also Nipal to Burma. IV—VII. **E. nuda,** Lindley.

3. Leaves present at flowering time .. **4**

Leaves absent at flowering time or entirely absent **5**

4. Height of the entire plant 120—220 cm.; leaves about three, linear, 30—110 cm. long, 2.5—5 cm. broad; flowers deflexed, yellow, 25 mm. across; petals broad-elliptic, streaked dull-brown; lip saccate at the base; side-lobes erect, blunt at the tip, end-lobe round, crenate-wavy, with nine thickened nerves.

Tropical valleys; also Upper Assam. VII, VIII. **E. Mannii,** Hooker fil.

— Flowering scape about 45 cm. long; leaves two, arising close to the scape, with the stalk about 100 cm. long, forming at the base a false stem; flowers 6—8, forming a loose raceme, spreading or half-erect, about 25 mm. across; sepals brown, the broad-oblong, connivent petals and the lip pale-yellow; lip oblong with two long and low side-lobes, 3—5 thickened nerves tuberculated at their outer ends and a short thick spur suddenly bent nearly at right-angles.

Tista valley, 1,000′. VIII. **E. geniculata,** King and Pantling.

5. Lip with a short, straight, narrow-cylindric spur, three parallel strong ridges ending in a patch of densely crowded short bristles on the transversely oblong, irregularly dentate end-lobe; raceme 6—9 cm. long; leaves two, linear, 25—40 cm. long; 1 cm. broad; flowers pale-pink with darker lines.

Terai and Duars, 6—1,000′; also Plains and Deccan. III. **E. campestris,** Wallich.

— Lip slightly saccate, never truly spurred .. **6**

6. Lip shorter than the sepals, space between the side-lobes with two granular lamellæ; end-lobe ovate-triangular; flowers dull-brown, nearly 4 cm. across; leaves probably totally absent.

Mangpu, 2,000′; also Khasia. V, VI.

E. sanguinea, Hooker fil.

— Lip longer than the sepals; end-lobe transversely oblong; sepals and petals pale yellowish-green, end-lobe of lip with a pale-purplish edge; basal part of lip with two ridges ending in a tooth **7**

7. Flowers about 2.5 cm. across; middle part of lip with about five tuberculate ridges of unequal length.

Foot of hills. III, IV.

E. bicarinata, Hooker fil. *var.* **genuina.**

— Flowers about 3 cm. across; middle part of lip with 10—13 close-set tuberculate ridges of nearly equal length.

Foot of hills. III, IV.

E. bicarinata, Hooker fil. *var.* **maior**, King and Pantling.

GEODORUM, Jackson.

1. Tuber globular, about 3 cm. in diameter; leaves elliptic, acute, 15—30 cm. long, 8—10 cm. broad; their sheaths forming a false stem from the side of the base of

which rises the scape: upper part of scape bent over and ending in a short corymb of flowers, but lengthening and becoming straight in fruit; parts of flowers erect; lip resembling a vessel with a spout, middle part granulated; flowers pure white or pale purple, lip with darker markings.

At low levels; widely distributed in India. IV, V. **G. purpureum,** R. Brown.

CREMASTRA, Lindley.

Tuber large, covered with nodules, producing a tall and erect stem bulbous at the base; leaves long-petioled, blade elliptic, plaited, 15—30 cm. long; inflorescences one or two, raceme conical, 10—15 cm. long; flowers pink, densely crowded, drooping, 30—35 mm. long; parts nearly erect; lip resembling a spoon with a long handle, end-lobe with a fleshy, basal appendage.

6—8,000′; also Nipal and Khasia. IV. **C. Wallichiana,** Lindley.

OREORCHIS, Lindley.

1. Corm ovoid, about 15 mm. long; leaf solitary, terminal, broad-lanceolate, 10—22 cm. long; scape from the side of the corm slender, raceme lax; flowers 13 mm. long; lip deflexed from the middle, with a globose small sack at the base, claw rather long, end-lobe obovate, emarginate, with five strong nerves; flowers reddish.

   Lachen valley, 10,000′; also Simla and Garhwal. **O. foliosa,** Lindley.

— Corm ovoid-conical, about 18 mm. long; leaves usually two, linear, 15—30 cm. long, commonly 6—10 mm. broad; scape from the side of the corm, slender; raceme lax; flowers 10 mm. long; lip obovate-oblong, only the bilobulate, red-spotted end-lobe deflexed; space between the side-lobes with a linear thick channelled swelling; flowers pale yellow.

Lachen valley, 10,000′; also Western Himalaya. **O. micrantha,** Lindley.

CYMBIDIUM, Swartz.

1. Terrestrial; inflorescence erect .. **2**

— Epiphytic; inflorescence decurved .. **4**

2. Roots long, thick and spongy; stems narrowly spindle-shaped, 5—15 cm. long, bearing 3—4 oblanceolate leaves at their upper end; leaf-blade 15—20 cm. long; inflorescence from the base of the stem; peduncle 5—8 cm. long; flowers 3—4, distant, about 4, rarely 5 cm. across; sepals and petals green, petals with a red median stripe; lip 3-lobed, white with red transverse bars.

Sureil, 6,000′; also Nipal to Khasia, and Perak. VI. **C. lancifolium,** Hooker.

— Roots solid; stem hardly any; leaves six and more, basal, linear, 22—90 cm. long; inflorescence about 30 cm. long; flowers fragrant **3**

8

3\. Flowers about 38 mm. across; green, later on yellowish; end-lobe of lip ovate or ovate-oblong, abruptly deflexed, lip with **purple markings.**

— Chungtang, 5,000′; also Garhwal to Shan Hills and in Perak. XI.

C. cyperifolium, Wallich.

— Flowers about 25 mm. across; sepals and petals straw-coloured with streaked or dotted purple lines; lip pink, end-lobe narrow, recurved, pale-yellow blotched with red.

Tista valley, on dry knolls, 1,500′; also Bhotan Duars. V.

C. Munronianum, King and Pantling.

4\. Inflorescence with 8 and more flowers .. **5**

— Inflorescence with 2 to 6 flowers .. **15**

5\. The parts of the flowers spreading or at first sub-erect, but finally spreading .. **6**

— The parts of the flowers nearly erect during the whole of the flowering period **13**

6\. Flowers less than 5 cm. across .. **7**

— Flowers, when fully open, more than 5 cm. across **10**

7\. Leaves long-petioled; petiole 12—20 cm. long; blade broadly oblanceolate 22—30 cm. long; 3.5—5 cm. broad; flowers 18 and more, about 3 cm. from the tip of dorsal sepal to tip of lip, less horizontally; lip decurved from the very base; sepals and petals purplish-brown with green lines, lip with a white patch mottled with purple near the base.

5—7,000′. V, VI. **C. devonianum,** Paxter.

— Leaves without a petiole, linear; only the end-lobe of the lip decurved 8

8. Flowers about 20; leaves broad-linear, 18—30 mm. broad 9

— Flowers 10—12; leaves narrow-linear, 90 cm. long and more, 10—13 mm. broad; lamellæ of lip thick, beset with glandular hairs; end-lobe ovate; sepals and petals white with a crimson middle line, lip white, lateral lobes marked with oblique yellow lines, end-lobe with a yellow blotch; flowers sweet-scented.

Tista valley, 1,000′; also Assam. VIII.
C. Simonsianum, King and Pantling.

9. Leaves 30—55 cm. long; 25—30 mm. broad; not attenuated towards the notched tip; peduncle of inflorescence at first ascending, passing into the deflexed axis of the lax raceme; flowers about 38 mm. across; lip oblong, with two lamellæ notched at the middle, end-lobe ovate-oblong, with a white patch at its base; lip otherwise purple with darker lines; sepals and petals yellowish.

At lower levels; also Assam, Bengal and elsewhere. IV, V. **C. aloifolium,** Swartz

— Leaves 60—80 cm. long; 18—25 mm. broad, somewhat narrower towards the acute tip; peduncle deflexed from its very base; flowers about 30 mm. across; lip sub-saccate at its base, end-lobe truncate, emarginate; flowers dark purple-brown, sepals and petals with a yellow edge; lamellæ continuous.

Bottom of tropical valleys and foot of hills; also Assam, Bengal, Burma, S. India and Andamans. V. **C. pendulum,** Swartz.

10. Flowers 7.5—10 cm. in diameter; petals and sepals apple-green, not longitudinally striped with brown; leaves broad-linear, expanded towards the base, 40—60 cm. long, 18—25 mm. broad; scape and raceme together 60—125 cm. long; space between the two side-lobes of the lip with two parallel hairy ridges, end-lobe emarginate, edges irregularly wavy; lip and column ochre-yellow speckled purple; lip and column red after fertilisation.

5—7,000′; also Nipal and Bhotan. II.
C. grandiflorum, Griffith.

— Flowers 6—7.5 cm. across; sepals and petals pale-green or of yellow tints, with longitudinal brown stripes or lines .. **11**

11. Leaves linear, 1—2 cm. broad; 60—90 cm. long; end-lobe of lip sub-orbicular, side-lobes with acute end pointing forwards .. **12**

— Leaves oblanceolate, 3—4 cm. broad, less than 50 cm. long; end-lobe of lip ovate-oblong, rather acute, margin wavy-crenate, side-lobes ovate with obtuse end; flowers ochre-yellow with brown lines, lip with brown transverse blotches; outer surface of sepals flushed green.

4—6,000′; also Kumaon to Khasia. X, XI. **C. giganteum,** Wallich.

12. Sepals oblong, dorsal sepal incurved; ground-colour of sepals and petals pale-green, with brownish-purple stripes; middle part and end-lobe of lip pure-white with purple spots, side-lobes ochre-coloured with numerous purple lines.

5—7,000′; also Garhwal to Khasia. IX, X. **C. longifolium,** Don.

— Sepals linear-oblanceolate, dorsal sepal erect; sepals and petals dirty-yellow or pale-yellow flushed with brown and marked with brown lines, lip brighter yellow with brown lines on the side-lobes.

5—7,000′. IX, X.
C. Gammieanum, King and Pantling.

13. Inflorescence from the base of the stem; flowers 10—12, forming a somewhat lax raceme; sepals and petals profusely spotted with dull-red on a pale yellowish-green ground; lip white or pale-pink, side- and end-lobes spotted pale-red, middle part of lip with two pubescent lamellæ.

Gantok, 5,000′. XI.
C. Whiteae, King and Pantling.

— Inflorescence axillary; flowers 12 to more than 20; sepals and petals not spotted .. **14**

14. Basal part of plant largely made up of the closely packed sheaths of fallen leaves (usually more than 10), about 12—15 cm. long; raceme obconical in outline, somewhat lax; flowers 20 or less; sepals and petals oblanceolate and blunt, dull-brown flushed with green: lip with side-lobes acute at their outer ends, ridges without a basal swelling, end-lobe triangular, straight, lip ochre-yellow dotted brown.

4—6,000′; also Assam and Khasia. X, XI.

C. cochleare, Lindley.

— Basal part of plant with loosely packed sheaths (about 10), 10 cm. and less long; raceme oblong-ellipsoidal in outline, very dense; flowers more than 20; sepals and petals narrow-oblong somewhat oblanceolate, acute, pale lemon-yellow, sometimes flushed with pink or brown, lamellæ of lip deeper yellow; flowers rarely white; end-lobe of lip incurved.

5—6,000′; also Nipal to Khasia. X, XI.

C. elegans, Lindley.

15. Leaves 15—18 mm. broad; raceme somewhat decurved; flowers 4—6, crowded; sepals and petals lanceolate, about 5 cm. long, white flushed pink upwards; lip narrow-oblong, side-lobes long and low with acute outer ends, mid-lobe suborbicular, lamellæ orange, lip yellowish outside.

5—7,000′; also Khasia. X, XI.

C. Mastersii, Griffith.

— Leaves 6—13 mm. broad; raceme straight; flowers 1—2, distant when two; sepals and petals oblong; 3.5—5 cm. long; white, dorsal sepal concave; lip obovate, side-lobes obscure, end-lobe triangular with wavy margin and a yellow patch, middle part of lip with a brilliant yellow, 3-ridged band; flowers sweet-scented.

1,000—3,000′, common; also from Nipal to Khasia. III, IV. **C. eburneum,** Lindley.

PHALÆNOPSIS, Blume.

1. Leaves elliptic, 7—13 cm. long, 3—4 cm. broad; raceme short, erect, 4—6-flowered; flowers 20—25 mm. across; sepals broadly ovate; petals blunt; end-lobe of lip reniform; flowers white, the lip with a chestnut band.

Tista valley, 1,200′, common; also from Bhotan to the Malay Archipelago. III, IV. **Ph. Parishii,** Reichenbach fil.

— Leaves elliptic-oblong, 12—40 cm. long, 5—10 cm. broad; raceme pendulous, as long as the leaves, lax, many-flowered; flowers 25—30 mm. across; lateral sepals oblanceolate, acute; end-lobe of lip broadly arrow-shaped; sepals and petals yellow with brown markings; lip ochraceous, marked purple near its base.

Tista valley, at lower levels, common; also Assam. V.

Ph. Mannii, Reichenbach fil.

DORITIS, Lindley.

1. Roots much shorter than the leaves; leaves about three, pendulous, broadly oblanceolate, blunt, 15—20 cm. long, 3—5 cm. broad; inflorescence pendulous; flowers about 15 mm. across; lateral sepals obliquely truncate; basal part of lip forming a wide-conical sack; flowers pale ochre-coloured with purple markings.

Tista valley at low levels; also Bhotan to Burma, and Malābar and Ceylon. VII.

D. Wightii, Bentham.

Roots flat, long, forming a spreading tuft; leaves one or a few, pendulous, broad-lanceolate, 7—13 cm. long; 15—20 mm. broad; inflorescence pendulous, somewhat exceeding the leaves; flowers about 20 mm. across; lateral sepals elliptic, blunt; basal part of lip produced into an irregularly conical spur; flowers pale-purple, or white changing into yellow, end-lobe of lip dark purple.

3—6,000′; also Kumaon to Burma. V.

D. tænialis, Bentham.

BIERMANNIA, King and Pantling.

Leaves 3—4, on a very short stem, fleshy, about 5 cm. long and 1 cm. broad; raceme short, few-flowered; flowers about 1 cm. in diameter, white; lip with two narrow side-lobes, a triangular end-lobe and two brown blotches on the fleshy swellings.

Tista valley, 1,500′. VII.

B. bimaculata, King and Pantling.

ORNITHOCHILUS, Wallich.

Stem very short; leaves broadly oblong, 7—15 cm. long; 3—5 cm. broad; inflorescence pendulous, much longer than the leaves; raceme lax, many-flowered; flowers 1 cm. across; sepals spreading; lip much longer than the sepals, the broad claw with a bent cylindric spur at right-angles to it, side-lobes subquadrate, end-lobe with two recurved and pectinate side-lobules and a triangular entire infolded end-lobule; ground-colour of flower greenish-yellow, sepals and petals with brown bands, the pectinate margin of the side-lobules brown passing into purple.

4—6,000′ also from Garhwal to Burma. VII, VIII. **O. fuscus,** Wallich.

LUISIA, Gaudichaud.

1. Stem pendulous, 60—150 cm. long; upwards 5 mm. and less thick; leaves one-sidedly inserted, 15—20 cm. long; about 3 mm. thick; internodes about 5 cm. long; flowers in clusters of 3 or 4, expanding one at a time; flowers from tip of dorsal sepal to tip of lip about 20 mm. in diameter; petals ultimately lengthening to about 25 mm., very narrowly linear and subspatulate; lip a little longer than the sepals, about 12 mm. long, basal part trapezoidal, end-part ovate, cordate, wavy, with rounded ridges above the basal part; sepals and petals pale-green; lip either

pale-green, or purplish-brown, margin of end-lobe usually pale-green.

Lower levels; also Khasia. III, IV.

L. volucris, Lindley.

— Stem erect, 30 cm. and less long; leaves spirally arranged, 15 cm. and less long; flowers 12 mm. and less from tip of dorsal sepal to tip of lip; petals not much longer than the sepals **2**

2. Lip not differentiated into basal and apical parts, broadly oblong, not furrowed; stem 12—18 cm. long; about 5 mm. thick; leaves slender, 11—15 cm. long; flowers pale-green, in clusters of 4—5; petals falcate.

Foot of Hills. III.

L. indivisa, King and Pantling.

— Lip differentiated into basal and apical parts **3**

3. Stems slender, flexous, 3 mm. thick: leaves aggregated near the upper end of the stem, 32—62 mm. long, less than 3 mm. thick; flowers 1—3, clustered, pale yellowish-green; basal part of lip hemispherically saccate, apical part subreniform, with 5—6 longitudinal lines.

Low levels; also Assam. VI, VII.

L. inconspicua, Hooker fil.

— Stems at least 5 mm. thick; leaves 62—180 mm. long, near the base at least 5 mm. thick; lip purple, end-lobe with 5—6 longitudinal rounded ridges .. **4**

4. Upper part of stem about 6 mm. thick; leaves tapering conspicuously from base to apex, 5 mm. thick at the base; basal part of lip square, somewhat saccate, apical lobe deflexed, rhomboid; sepals and petals green.

   Bottom of valleys and up to 3,000′; also widely distributed in India. V.

   L. teretifolia, Gaudichaud.

— Upper part of stem 8—10 mm. thick; leaves only slightly tapering from base to apex, thickest portion 5—6 mm.; basal part of lip squarish below and triangular upwards, deeply concave, apical part cordate, ovate, tapering to a short truncate apex; sepals pale-green with faint purple lines; ridges of apical part of lip pale-greenish.

   Low levels; also Garhwal. III, IV.

   L. trichorrhiza, Blume.

DIPLOPRORA, Hooker fil.

Epiphytic; stem pendulous, 7—15 cm. long, slender; leaves fleshy, oblong-lanceolate, 3.5—8.5 cm. long, 15—18 mm. broad; raceme 3—4-flowered, peduncle 12—25 mm. long; flowers 18 mm. across; sepals and petals yellow; lip white, basal part box-shaped, apical part triangular, laterally compressed, suddenly contracted to the two-tailed apex.

Bhotan, above Engo, 2,000′; also Mikir Hills, Khasia and Ceylon. VII, VIII.

D. Championi, Hooker fil.

STAUROPSIS, Reichenbach fil.

Epiphytic; stem erect, 20—35 cm. long, minutely warted; leaves oblanceolate, blunt and retuse, 7—10 cm. long, less than 2 cm. broad; flowers few, nearly 4 cm. across, on a spreading, extra-axillary 15—20 cm. long peduncle; sepals and petals more or less reflexed, wavy, fleshy, white flushed with pink; lip yellowish-green striped with pink, the basal part with large, erect auricles, apical part concave, median band with two ridges.

5—7,000′; also Bhotan and Khasia. IV, V. **St. undulata,** Bentham.

SARCOCHILUS, R. Brown.

1. Stem and leaves absent; inflorescence a pendulous, 7—37 cm. long, lax raceme, flowers 5—20, nearly sessile, rather distant, about 13 mm. across, sepals and petals yellow with brown spots; lip jointed to the foot, forming a deep triangular pouch, with large side-lobes and a knob-like end-lobe; lip yellow with brown bands.

Tropical valleys; also Burma. V.
S. luniferus, Bentham.

Stem about 2.5 cm. long, pendulous; leaves linear-lanceolate, 4—8 cm. long; inflorescence 3.5—4 cm. long, 2—3-flowered; flowers about 8 mm. across; lip adnate to the foot, forming a 2-grooved pouch with large side-lobes, apical lobe reduced to a bilobed thickening.

Pamiongtsi, 3,000′. IV.

S. pygmaeus. King and Pantling.

ARACHNANTHE, Blume.

1. Leaves oblong-linear, about 2 cm. broad. 6—11 times as long as broad; flowers 2—4 cm. in diameter; sepals and petals pale-yellow with dark-brown markings; lip white soon becoming yellow with pink lines on the six narrow ridges, and with a blunt cylindric spur about the middle of its lower surface.

Bhotan, Rumpti valley at lower levels; also Assam and Khasia. VIII.

A. bilinguis, Bentham.

- Leaves oblong, 3.5—4.5 cm. broad, 3.5—4.5 times as long as broad; flowers 4.5 to 8 cm. in diameter; lip without a spur on its lower surface, but only with a slight protrusion 2

2. Sepals and petals elliptic-oblong or obovate-oblong, one and a half to twice as long as broad, almost white outside, upper surface chocolate-brown with many yellow transverse bars; lip white outside, the basal part and a broad edge of the apical part yellow, the former and its auricles marked with pink; the median zone of the latter with 3—5 ridges.

3—6,000′, by the sides of streams; also Bhotan. III, IV. **A. Cathcartii,** Bentham.

— Sepals and petals oblanceolate, lateral sepals more distinctly so and falcate, all of them white outside, upper surface gamboge-yellow with broad irregular chestnut-brown transverse stripes, upper surface of apical part of lip deeply furrowed.

6—8,000′; also Bhotan. XI.

A. Clarkei, Rolfe.

AERIDES, Loureiro.

1. Leaves terete; stem slender; peduncle extra-axillary, bearing one or two flowers **2**

— Leaves strap-shaped; stem stout, erect or ascending, more than 1 cm. thick; inflorescence a many-flowered raceme .. **3**

2. Stem pendulous, about 3 mm. thick; leaves 10—18 cm. long, slender-awl-shaped, about 2 mm. greatest thickness; flowers about 2 cm. across, white; lobes of lip small; spur narrowly funnel-shaped, white with a pink flush.

Bhotan, at Dumsong, 5,500′; also Nipal, Upper Assam, Naga Hills. IX.

A. longicornu, Hooker fil

— Stem ridged, up to 20 cm. long; leaves 6—10 cm. long, thick, slightly tapering to a point; flowers creamy white with purple markings; lip with deep-purple spots on the under surface and bright yellow spots above, side-lobes large, obliquely oblong, end-lobe fleshy, ridged down the centre; spur purple.

Bhotan. **A. Greenii,** W. W. Smith.

3. Leaves rather flat, broad-oblong, the lower ovate-oblong, breadth 2.5—4 cm.; peduncle inserted somewhat above the axil of its leaf, deflexed nearly from its base; flowers white with many pink spots, very fragrant; spur large, funnel-shaped, strongly curved forwards.

Foot of hills and up to 3,000′; also Nipal to Burma. V, VI. **A. odoratum,** Lourier.

Leaves folded in, broadly linear, breadth 18—30 mm.; peduncle axillary, at first ascending; flowers white, freely marked pink or purple; lip twice as long as the sepals, basal part thick, spur short and wide-conical, apical part triangular.

Tropical valleys; also Assam. IV.
A. multiflorum, Roxburgh.

RHYNCHOSTYLIS, Blume.

Stem stout, ascending, clothed with the sheaths of fallen leaves below and bearing numerous, crowded leaves above; leaves broadly linear, curved, sides folded in, length 15—50 cm., breadth about 2.5 cm.; flowers 18 mm. across, very many, on an elongated pendulous raceme; the basal part of the lip forming a wide and deep sack, the apical part obovate, acute with erect margins; flowers white or purple, variously marked with purple or violet.

Tropical valleys and up to 3,500′; also Garhwal to Burma, and Southern India and Ceylon. **Rh. retusa,** Blume.

VANDA, R. Brown.

1. Leaves flat, folded in; stem not exceeding 30 cm. in length; apical lobe of lip oblong or ovate-oblong 2

Leaves fleshy, terete, slightly tapering to the obtuse tip, greatest thickness 4—6 mm.; stem 60—240 cm. in length, smooth; flowers 6—10 cm. across; sepals and petals rose-coloured, rarely white; lip with rounded side-lobes, a clawed obovate and bifid end-lobe and a wide-mouthed funnel-shaped yellow or ferruginous spur marked with purplish-brown lines.

Terai and hot valleys; also Assam to Upper Burma and Andamans and Nicobars. III, IV. **V. teres,** Lindley.

Sepals more than 15 mm. long, like the petals sub-erect, not widely spreading, the comparatively short peduncles arising in the axils of fresh leaves 3

Sepals about 6 mm. long, like the petals widely spreading, pale-buff; peduncles arising from the axils of the sheaths of leaves, about 2 mm. thick and about 5 cm.

long; lip with a funnel-shaped spur, bluish-purple, side-lobes rounded, end-lobe with two tubercles, fleshy lateral bands and a median groove.

Base of hills and bottom of hot valleys; also Kumaon to Burma, Western Ghats and Ceylon. IV—VI.

V. parviflora, Lindley.

3. Lip with a funnel-shaped spur 4

— Lip without a spur; flowers 1–2, greenish or yellowish, nodding sepals and petals slightly connivent, 15—18 mm. long; apical lobe of lip ovate-oblong, with some shallow ridges.

Tendong, 5,000′; also Garhwal to Khasia. VII. **V. alpina,** Lindley.

4. Flowers 2.5 cm. across; sepals and petals connivent; lip shorter than the sepals; end-lobe broadly ovate, with 4—6 thickened median ridges and two small knobs near the tip; flowers cream-coloured, lip longitudinally streaked red, sepals and petals speckled red.

Bottom of valleys. V.

V. pumila, Hooker fil.

— Flowers 2—5, 2.5—5 cm. across; sepals and petals half-erect, not connivent; lip longer than the sepals; end-lobe oblong, ending in two spreading lobules and a horn-like fleshy beak pointing downwards; upper surface with five tubercled ridges;

sepals and petals yellowish or olive-green, with purplish-brown blotches.

2—6,000, common; also Kumaon to Bhotan and in Sylhet. **V. cristata,** Lindley.

SACCOLABIUM.

1. Leaves not longer than 25 mm., lanceolate-ovate; stems slender, pendulous .. **2**

— Leaves longer, often much longer than 30 mm. **4**

2. Sepals and petals green flushed with brown, lip yellowish; spur dorsally compressed, shortly bilobed; apical lobe of lip broadly triangular, with two longitudinal weal-like ridges.

Eastern parts and western front of Sikkim, Pamionchi, 8,000′. VI.
S. affine, King and Pantling.

— Sepals and petals greenish with brown or brownish-purple spots; spur entire .. **3**

3. Apical lobe of lip orange; lip without any swelling.

6,000—8,000′; also in Khasia. VIII—X.
S. pseudo-distichum, King and Pantling.

— Apical lobe of lip pale-yellow; lip with two blunt conical swellings at its base.

6,000—8,000′. IV. V.
S. distichum, Lindley.

4. Stem more or less erect, not manifestly pendulous **5**

— Stem pendulous **8**

5. Inflorescences longer than the leaves; branches of the leaf-opposed inflorescences irregularly scattered, 1—6-flowered; stem 30—90 cm. long, stout; leaves oblong-linear, apex blunt, unequally shortly bilobed; sepals and petals yellow with brown markings, spur yellow, tubular, straight.

Sikkim, base of range and at the bottom of valleys; also in Bhotan, Khasia, Tenasserim, Ceylon. XI—XII.

S. ochraceum, Lindley.

— Inflorescences shorter than the leaves .. **6**

6. Inflorescences extra-axillary, usually leaf-opposed; flowers in terminal, few-flowered subcorymbose racemes; spur comparatively short, not longer than the sepals, conical, straight; leaves not mottled **7**

— Inflorescences from the axil of leaves; flowers many in an erect dense raceme; spur longer than the sepals, cylindrical, bent; leaves mottled with brown; stem stout, 8—14 cm. long; leaves narrowly oblong, unequally shortly bilobed; parts of flower of various pink shades, pollinia deep purple.

Sikkim, 1,000—3,000′, common; also Nipal, Sylhet, Khasia, Burma. III, IV.
S. ampullacaum, Lindley.

7. Stem 70 to 100 cm. long, very stout; leaves linear-oblong, 25—35 cm. long, rather flat; inflorescence consisting of a stout rather long peduncle and a few-flowered subcorymbose raceme; flowers about 13 mm. across; lip with side-lobes, terminal lobe with even edge.

Sikkim, along foot of hills and in tropical valleys; also upper Assam and Burma. VI.
S. longifolium, Hooker fil.

— Stem less than 50 cm. long, 10 mm. and less thick; leaves linear, 7—10 cm. long, distinctly conduplicate; inflorescence a 4—8-flowered subcorymbose raceme on a very short peduncle; flowers about 8 mm. across; lip without side-lobes, apical lobe white, undulate-crenate.

Sikkim, lower elevations; also Assam, Khasia, Chittagong, S. Bengal, Burma. X—I.
S. papillosum, Lindley.

8. Stems short, less than 10 cm. long; internodes very short and leaves crowded .. **9**

— Stems 10 cm. long and often considerably longer, internodes usually well developed and leaves commonly not conspicuously crowded **11**

9. Leaves less than 10 cm. long, linear-oblanceolate; inflorescence racemose; flowers cream-coloured, except at the entrance to the spur and the base of the apical lobe of the lip, where they are purplish; dorsal sepal oblanceolate-oblong, lateral elliptic; apical lobe of lip broad-triangular; spur tapering, longer than the ovary, curved forward.

Sikkim, about 1,500′; also Sylhet. IV.

S. pumilio, Reichenbach fil.

— Leaves more, often considerably more than 10 cm. long; inflorescence subcorymbose; flowers differently coloured; spur forming a wide sack **10**

10. Sepals and petals subequal; side-lobes of lip shallow; apical lobe semicircular, with laciniate edge and glabrous disc; sepals and petals bright-yellow with brownish purple spots; lip white with a patch of yellow sprinkled with brown spots near the apex and a purple edging to the sack.

Sikkim, valleys near the southern face of the hills; also Nipal and Assam. XI. XII.

S. dasypogon, Lindley.

— Sepals unequal, dorsal one obovate-oblong; side-lobes of lip absent; apical lobe semicircular, margin and most of the upper surface covered with white hair-like papillæ; sepals and petals green with brown markings; apical lobe of lip white with a yellow speckled pad near its base.

Sikkim, 4,000—6,000′; also Nipal, Garhwal, Khasia. III. IV. **S. calceolare,** Lindley.

11. Lip expanded into a wide sack .. **12**

— Lip distinctly spurred **13**

12. Leaves linear, length ten to twenty times the breadth; umbel 3- 4-flowered, about the length of the leaf-sheath; dorsal sepal broader; apical lobe of lip semicircular, minutely papillose, edges with a fringe of white fimbriæ; flowers yellow, spotted brownish-purple.

Sikkim, on the Nipal frontier, 3,000′; also Khasia, 3,000—5,000′. VIII.
S. intermedium, Griffith.

— Leaves oblong-lanceolate, four to six times as broad; umbels 6—8-flowered; peduncle much longer than the leaf-sheaths; sepals and petals subequal; apical lobe of lip kidney-shaped; edges fimbriate; a fleshy glabrous, heart-shaped cushion in the lower middle, otherwise papillose on the upper surface; sepals and petals either pale-green flushed and mottled with brown, or uniformly yellow; lip white, the fleshy disc bright yellow with dull-red spots.

Sikkim, 3,000′; also Khasia. XI, XII.
S. acutifolium, Lindley.

13. Spur nearly straight **14**

— Spur conspicuously curved **15**

14. Stem 30 cm. or less long; leaves narrow-oblong, five to nine times as long as broad; inflorescences leaf-opposed, longer than their leaves, densely racemose; petals much smaller than the sepals; spur bottle-shaped with contracted neck and globose apex; side-lobes of lip spreading, apical lobe narow-oblong.

Sikkim, about 2,000′; also Bhotan, Assam, Sylhet, Tenasserim. V, VI.

S. buccosum, Reichenbach fil.

— Stem 30—100 cm. long; leaves narrow-oblong, nine to twelve times as long as broad; inflorescences supra-axillary; much shorter than the leaves, one-sided, few-flowered; petals slightly shorter but broader than the sepals; spur with two swellings half-way down the tube, cylindrical, slightly recurved; side-lobes of lip erect, broadly triangular; apical lobe short, triangular, acute.

Sikkim, 1,000—2,500′, common; also in Bhotan and Assam. VII, VIII.

S. trichromum, Reichenbach fil.

— Sepals and petals pale-straw-coloured with a middle pale-pink band; spur rose-coloured, column white.

15. Stem 10—15 cm. long, comparatively stout; leaves linear-oblong, 15—20 cm. long, six to eight times as long as broad; inflorescences leaf-opposed or infra-axillary, longer than the leaves, forming

a dense many-flowered, strict raceme; spur funnel-shaped, body wide, much curved, apex bulbous; apical lobe of lip thick, laterally compressed, 3-lobulate; flowers pale-yellow.

Sikkim, 3,500—5,000′; also in Bhotan and Khasia. IX, X. **S. obtusifolium,** Hooker fil.

— Stems slender, 15—30 cm. long; inflorescences shorter than the neighbouring leaves; spur not bulbous at the apex **16**

16. Leaves ovate- or elliptic-lanceolate, acute, 4—6 cm. long, about six times as long as broad; racemes leaf-opposed, 8—12-flowered; side-lobes of lip conspicuous, erose, apical lobe fleshy, broad-triangular; flowers pale-green, anterior lobe of lip and the tips of the petals whitish.

Sikkim, 6,000—7,000′, rare; in Khasia common. VII—IX.
S. acuminatum, Hooker fil.

— Leaves linear, 20—30 cm. long, drawn out into a point, 12—16 times as long as broad; racemes axillary, much shorter than their leaf, densely flowered; side-lobes of lip absent, lip boat-shaped with fleshy apex.

Sikkim, at Rissisum, 6,000′. VI.
S. lancifolium, King and Pantling.

CLEISOCENTRON, P. Brühl.

Stem 30—100 cm. long, pendulous; leaves narrow-oblong, 9—12 times as long as broad; inflorescence supra-axillary. much shorter than the leaves, one-sided. few-flowered; sepals and petals pale straw-coloured with a middle pink band; spur rose-coloured; column white; side-lobes of lip erect, broadly triangular; end-lobe short, triangular.

1,000—2,500′. common; also Bhotan and Assam. VII, VIII.

Cl. trichromum, (Reichenbach fil.).

The same as S. trichromum on page 135.

CLEISOSTOMA, Blume.

1. Leaves strap-shaped or linear-oblong, four to seven times as long as broad. apex obliquely bilobed or truncate **2**

   Leaves semiterete. ovate-lanceolate or linear, six to twenty-five times as long as broad. apex acute. mucronate or minutely dentate **4**

2. Stem hardly any; inflorescences axillary. usually three-branched; spur wide, sub-globose; apical lobe of lip fleshy. reniform; flowers pale-yellow. neck of spur flushed with pink.

   Sikkim, tropical valleys. ascending to 1500′; also in Kachar. Tenasserim and Andamans. VI, VI.

   Cl. Wendlandorum, Reichenbach fil.

   Stem elongate, six to forty cm. long; inflorescences leaf-opposed; spur funnel-shaped or short-cylindric. at the apex bulb-like or even **3**

3. Leaves 3—4 cm. broad, rather flat; inflorescences longer than the leaves, forming dense racemes; spur three-notched at the apex; flowers yellow, mottled and banded brown-purple, column white.

Tista valey, 1,000′; also Tenasserim. VI.
Cl. spicatum, Lindley.

— Leaves 1.2 to 1.5 cm. broad, somewhat conduplicate; inflorescences shorter than the leaves, flowers many, but only a few expanding at a time; spur not notched; sepals and petals white with pink spots, lip pink or purple.

Sikkim, 2,000—3,000′; also from Dehra Dun to Naga and Khasia Hills and in Tenasserim. VII, VIII.
Cl. micranthum, King and Pantling.

4. Leaves lanceolate, acute, 9—13 mm. broad; stem pendulous, branching; spikes extra-axillary, much shorter than the leaves; spur a short, wide sack; apical lobe of lip fleshy, hastate, with a narrow decurved apex running out into two short awns; sepals and petals yellow with brown bands; lip pale-buff, apical lobe white.

Sikkim, tropical valleys; also in Assam. VIII. **Cl. brevipes,** Hooker fil.

— Leaves linear or semiterete 5

5. Stems erect, rigid, 5—10 cm. long; leaves semiterete, mucronate; flowers

in small crowded heads; spur wide-conical; flowers pale straw-coloured flushed with pink.

Sikkim, at low elevations; common. IX.

Cl. armigerum, King and Pantling.

— Stems or inflorescence pendulous, leaves linear, not mucronate; flowers in racemes or panicles 6

6. Stems hardly any, the leaves forming a hanging cluster, straight or slightly curved; inflorescences a strict, about 12-flowered raceme; spur funnel-shaped; apical lobe of lip triangular-ovate, acute; dorsal sepal outside brown flushed with yellow, inside buff-coloured; lateral sepals and petals buff, lip buff on upper surface, side-lobes with brown streaks, a yellow patch on the apical lobe.

On the nodes of bamboos, in Bhotan, at Rumpti Lake, 1,500′. V.

Cl. bambusarum, King and Pantling.

Stems slender with well-developed internodes; leaves narrow-linear, falcately curved, margins infolded, with minutely 3-toothed tip; inflorescence axillary, a panicle of usually three racemes; spur nearly cylindric; apical lobe of lip ovate-rotund, blunt; flowers purple except the white apical lobe of the lip and the inner surface of the petals.

Sikkim, 2,000—3,000′, common; also in Bhotan, Khasia, Jaintia. VII, VIII.

Cl. gemmatum, King and Pantling.

STEREOCHILUS, Lindley.

1. Stem at right-angles to the substratum, increasing in thickness upwards, glabrous; leaves linear-oblong, irregularly bilobulate, 8—15 cm. long, 20—25 mm. broad, rather flat; inflorescence usually somewhat longer than the leaves, pendulous, sparsely flowered, often slightly branched, peduncle and axis of raceme glabrous, about 2 mm. thick; flowers about 8 mm. across; lip with a blunt, cylindrical spur; end-lobe ovate; sepals and petals yellowish, pink along the midrib.

   2,000′; also Khasia and Tenasserim. VII, VIII. **St. bicuspidatus,** King and Pantling.

— Stem erect, cylindric; the peduncle and axis of the decurved inflorescence covered with glandular hairs; leaves fleshy, semiterete, deeply grooved, 8—13 cm. long, about 12 mm. broad; racemes axillary about 10-flowered, lax, decurved, distinctly longer than the leaves; flowers about 18 mm. across; lip with a wide-conical, sack-like, basal spur, triangular connivent side-lobes and a concave, ovate-oblong, blunt end-lobe; sepals and petals pink, lip white and pink.

   Tendong, 6,000′; also Khasia and Tenasserim. VI. **St. hirtus,** Lindley.

CAMAROTIS, Lindley.

1. Stem erect, about 7 mm. thick; leaves about at right-angles to the stem,

narrowly lanceolate; racemes leaf-opposed; flowers about 18 mm. across; lip resembling a pouch with a slanting opening; lateral sepals adhering for part of their length to the lip; the latter divided into an upper and a lower chamber; flowers white, lip with a yellow spot.

Tropical valleys; also Tenasserim. VIII.

C. obtusa, Lindley.

— Stem pendulous, about 4 mm. thick; leaves at an angle of about 45° to the stem, linear; racemes between the leaves; flowers about 6 mm. across; lip resembling a pouch with a square opening; sepals and petals free; lip not divided clearly into an upper and lower chamber; flowers pale pink with crimson spots.

Tista valley, 1,200′. VI, VII.

C. Mannii, King and Pantling.

SARCANTHUS, Lindley.

1. Leaves terete **2**

— Leaves flat **3**

2. Stem erect, 20—40 cm. long, flexuous; leaves spirally arranged, ascendant, 7—10 cm. long; inflorescence decurved, longer than the leaves; flowers 15 mm. long; sepals and petals spreading, buff with purple longitudinal lines; lip with a basal, stout-cylindrical spur with two

swellings near its mouth, end-lobe fleshy, decurved, triangular, pink or pale-lavender.

Tropical valleys; also Assam, Burma, Mysore. VIII.

S. appendiculatus, Hooker fil.

— Stem pendulous, 25—180 cm. long; leaves mostly on one side, 20—25 cm. long; inflorescence arising between the leaves, pendulous, shorter than the leaves; flowers about 11 mm. long; sepals and petals reflexed, brown, edges and midribs yellow or buff; lip with a basal compressed, sack-like spur, end-lobe small, triangular, white flushed pink; interior of spur 2-celled.

Tropical valleys, common; also Khasia and Burma. VIII, IX. **S. filiformis,** Lindley.

3. Stem erect, short and stout; leaves close-set from the base upwards, strap-shaped, 20—30 cm. long, 33—40 mm. broad; inflorescence an axillary panicle, much exceeding the leaves, consisting of spreading, straight or incurved many-flowered racemes; flowers 10—13 mm. across; sepals and petals spreading, dull-brown edged with yellow, lip fleshy, white, longer than the sepals, with a basal, thick-cylindric spur, end-lobe fleshy, ovate; spur divided into two collateral chambers.

2,000—4,000′; also Nipal to Burma. VIII.

S. pallidus, Lindley

— Stem pendulous, 15—30 cm. long; about 3 mm. thick; leaves linear-lanceolate,

6—10 cm. long; 5—9 mm. broad; racemes pendulous, contracted, less than 25 mm. long; flowers about 6 mm. across; sepals and petals spreading, yellow with intra-marginal brown bands; lip fleshy, with a swollen short-cylindric spur with an internal septum; basal part of lip white, end-lobe pink.

Base of hills and lower part of hot valleys; also Sylhet, Assam, Khasia and Chittagong. **S. secundus,** Griffith.

DENDROCOLLA, Blume.

Stem erect, rigid, 15—20 cm. long; bearing 6—8, horizontally spreading, narrow-oblong, 7—10 cm. long and 15—18 mm. broad leaves and emitting numerous slender roots; flowers short-lived, about 25 mm. across; sepals and petals linear-lanceolate, acuminate, 3 cm. long, yellow; lip speckled red, much shorter than the petals, with a basal, wide-conical spur and an oblong, tumid end-lobe; bracts persistent; the raceme continues growing for several years.

Bhotan, foot of range; also Assam to Penang. IX. **D. Arachnites,** Blume.

ORNITHARIUM, Lindley.

Stem 7—15 cm. long, about 6 mm. thick, pendulous; leaves strap-shaped, close-set, stem-clasping, 9—18 cm. long, 16—23 mm.

broad; racemes pendulous, leaf-opposed, longer than the leaves, lengthening during the flowering season, which extends considerably; flowers about 13 mm. in diameter; sepals and petals yellow with brown spots; lip nearly entirely made up of the narrowly funnel-shaped spur ending in a slightly bulbous tip, side- and end-lobes very small, upper surface white, tip of lip dark-purple.

Tropical valleys; also Chittagong and Tenasserim. **O. striatulum,** Lindley.

TÆNIOPHYLLUM, Blume.

1. Roots about 5 mm. thick; stem about 18 mm. high; flowers 1—2, green, 5 mm. long; sepals and petals narrow-lanceolate, spreading; lip narrow-lanceolate with a basal, sub-globose spur and an apical inflexed tooth.

5,000′. VI.

T. retrospiculatum, King and Pantling.

Roots 2 mm. thick; raceme about 9 mm. long; flowers in two rows opening singly, 3 mm. long; sepals ovate, incurved, greenish like the lanceolate petals; lip cup-like, white, with an ellipsoidal spur.

Tropical valleys. IX.

T. crepidiforme, King and Pantling.

PODOCHILUS, Blume.

1. Stems about 15 cm. long, densely covered with equitant, ovate-oblong, acute, about

17 mm. long leaves; flowers 2—4, about 5 mm. long, white flushed pink; sepals free; lip gibbous at the base, oblong.

2—3,000′, common; also from Nipal to Burma. IX. X. **P. cultratus,** Lindley.

— Stems 10—15 cm. long, slender; leaves somewhat remote from each other, linear-lanceolate, slightly tapering towards their base, 8—15 mm. long; flowers 3—4, about 3.7 mm. long, white flushed yellow; lateral sepals connate below into a short pouch; lip arrow-shaped and clawed at the base, acute.

Sittang, 5—6,000′. IX.

P. khasianus, Hooker fil.

RISLEYA, King and Pantling.

Scape 5—13 cm. high; with two basal sheaths; flowers minute, forming a dense 1.3—3 cm. long spike; flowers 1.5 mm. across, blackish-purple; lip ovate, very concave, with a minute apical point.

Jongri, 13,000′. VI, VII.

R. atropurpurea, King and Pantling.

CERATOSTYLIS, Blume.

Stems crowded. on a dense fibrous rhizome, terete, rush-like, sheathed at the base, and bearing at the upper end, jointed to it, a single terete awl-shaped leaf;

flowers 2.5 mm. long, forming a head sessile at the leaf-joint, 6—9 mm. in diameter; sepals and petals spreading, white; lip club-shaped with a long claw and a fleshy terminal yellow part.

Tista valley, 1,000′; also Upper Assam and Khasia. V, VI. **C. teres,** Reichenbach fil.

APPENDICULA, Blume.

Epiphytic; stems tufted, slender, unbranched, 25—60 cm. long; leaves numerous, in two rows, broad-lanceolate, 22—30 mm. long and 8—10 mm. broad; raceme mostly terminal, about 12 mm. long; 6—8-flowered; flowers white, flushed yellow; lip fleshy, oblong with a superposed appendix having a globular swelling near its apex.

Tropical valleys; also Kachar to Perak. VIII. **A. bifaria,** Lindley

THELASIS, Blume.

1. Pseudobulbs broad-ovoid, 10—17 mm. in diameter; leaves one or two, from the apex of the pseudobulb, linear-lanceolate, 2.5—8 cm. long; 5—12 mm. broad; scape rising from the base of the pseudobulb, longer than the leaves; raceme 12—25 mm. long; flowers crowded, 2—3 mm. long, pale green; lip oblong with small rounded basal side-lobes.

At low levels; also Malabar and Tenasserim. VIII, IX. **Th. pygmaea,** Lindley.

— Pseudobulbs broadly conical, 12—19 mm. long; leaf solitary from the apex of the pseudobulb, oblong or broad-lanceolate, 10—15 cm. long and 12—18 mm. broad; scape from a developing pseudobulb, somewhat longer than the leaves; raceme rather lax, 2.5—5 cm. long; flowers 5 mm. long, green; lip oblong-elliptic without side-lobes.

Tropical valleys; also Khasia. VII, VIII.
Th. longifolia, Hooker fil.

PHREATIA, Lindley.

Pseudobulbs tufted, compressed-ovoid, about 12 mm. long; leaves one to several, broad-lanceolate, 10—15 cm. long, about 2 cm. broad; inflorescence from among the leaves, erect, much longer than the leaves; raceme narrow-cylindrical, many-flowered; flowers 3 mm. across, white; sepals and petals spreading; lip oblong, deflexed at the middle, attached to the foot of the column.

Chungthang, 6.000′; also Khasia. VIII.
Ph. elegans, Lindley.

EPIPOGUM, Gmelin.

1. Root coralloid; stem less than 20 cm. high, about 5 mm. thick at the middle,

bearing two bracts at and below the middle and a raceme of about 4 flowers at the upper end; flowers ascending, about 18 mm. from tip of dorsal sepal to tip of lip; sepals and petals narrow oblong, erect; lip with large side-lobes, a deflexed, concave, ovate, longitudinally ridged end-lobe and a stout club-shaped, red-streaked spur about as long as the lip proper; whole plant faint yellowish.

Lachen valley, 12,000′; also westwards to Kashmir and beyond. IX.

E. aphyllum, Swartz.

— Tuber underground, 5 cm. and more in length; stem 10—40 cm. high; about 1 cm. thick at the base, gradually thinner upwards, with a few bracts and ending in a 5—20 cm. long raceme; flowers drooping, minus the ovary about 12 mm. long, white; sepals and petals lanceolate-linear, connivent; lip oblong, concave, without side-lobes but with a short blunt point, with a few reddish-brown spots; spur half as long as the lip, somewhat bulbous; stem and ovary pale-ochre-coloured.

Hot valleys up to 4,000′; also Nipal to Khasia, Deccan and Ceylon. IV—VI.

E nutans, Reichenbach fil.

LISTERA, R. Brown.

1. Leafless; stem 20—35 cm. high; bearing 3—4 tubular sheaths and terminating an elongated, many-flowered spike; flowers

8—13 mm. from tip of dorsal sepal to tip of lip; lip 2—3 times as long as the sepals, bilobulate, narrowed towards the base, with a lanceolate-linear thickening down the middle; flowers probably reddish-brown.

Lachen valley; 10,000′; also westwards to Kashmir. VII.

L. Lindleyana, King and Pantling.

— Stem leafy; leaves two; flowers green .. 2

2. Lip broader than long, pectinate-dentate, clawed, with a thickened median line; whole plant 20—30 cm. high; stem about 5 mm. thick; leaves opposite, orbicular, cordate, 25—38 mm. long, inserted just below the spike; flowers close-set, at least 30, about 7 mm. across; dorsal sepal and petals recurved.

Jongri, 13,000′. VII.

L. dentata, King and Pantling.

— Lip longer than broad, not clawed, lateral margins, entire; stem no more than 3 mm. thick; flowers less than 16 3

3. Lip squarish, with three acute, unequal lobules at the apex, the middle lobule the longest; stem 7—13 cm. high; leaves opposite, about 3 cm. above the base, orbicular-ovate, 7—13 mm. long; flowers 4—6 in a lax spike, pale green.

Lachen and Lachung Valleys, 10—11,000′. VII. **L. micrantha,** Lindley.

— Lip oblong or obovate, emarginate, obcordate or bilobed 4

4. Leaves close to the ground, roundish-ovate, 20—25 mm. long; inflorescence 14—24 cm. long, puberulous; flowers 12—16, scattered, about 8 mm. from tip of dorsal sepal to tip of lip, dull olive-green; lip fleshy, obcordate, with a thickened median brown line.

Lachen valley, 9,000′. VII.

L. brevicaulis, King and Pantling.

— Leaves inserted higher up 5

5. Flowers less than 8 mm. from tip of dorsal sepal to tip of lip; leaves opposite or alternate 6

— Flowers 12—25 mm. from tip of dorsal sepal to tip of lip; leaves opposite .. 7

6. Leaves alternate; whole plant 20—25 cm. high; peduncle puberulous; flowers 7—9, nodding, olive-green; sepals spreading, lanceolate; lip somewhat longer, obovate-oblong, emarginate, with a thickened narrowly linear median ridge.

Lachen valley, 10,000′. VII.

L. alternifolia, King and Pantling.

Leaves strictly opposite; whole plant 10—15 cm. high; raceme glandular-puberulous; sepals and petals connivent, oblong, pale olive-green; lip longer, pale-brown, obovate-wedge-shaped, shortly bilobed, with a dark midrib.

Lachen and Chumbi valleys, 11—12,000′. VII. **L. tenuis,** Lindley.

7. Leaves 12—25 mm. long; lip about twice as long as the dorsal sepal, obovate-oblong, pale-brown with a broad darker median band; sepals and petals pale olive-green; whole plant 10—20 cm. long; raceme 2—10-flowered.

Lachen and Chumbi valleys, 10—11,000′. VII. **L. pinetorum,** Lindley.

— Leaves 30—38 mm. long; lip about four times as long as the dorsal sepal, elliptic-oblong, like petals and sepals nearly uniformly green, veins darker, with a thickened median line; whole plant 15—35 cm. long; raceme 8—14-flowered.

Lachen valley, 7,000′. VII.

L. longicaulis, King and Pantling.

PANTLINGIA, Prain.

Rhizome about 3 cm. (or less) long; 3—6 mm. thick, horizontal, emitting one or two leafless stems, about 2 mm. thick, strict, erect, bearing a small bract at the middle and 2—3 pale yellow flowers at the upper end; flowers 3—4 mm. long (ovary 3—4 times longer); lateral sepals linear adpressed to the lip; petals reflexed or spreading; lip transversely elliptic, upper surface with two elongated parallel swellings, a basal two-lobed fleshy tongue-like process, and a purple patch at the middle.

Chungtong, 6,000′. IX. **P. paradoxa,** Prain.

GASTRODIA, R. Brown.

Rhizome short, 3—5 mm. thick, horizontal, emitting fibrous roots; stems erect, 30—45 cm. long, about 2 mm. thick, bearing at long intervals about 3 bracts and 3—4 distant, nodding, 12—15 mm. long, brown flowers; sepals connate into a cylindrical, irregularly swollen, 3-toothed tube; petals minute; lip yellowish-white, shorter than the sepaline tube, ovate-lanceolate, clawed, with crenulate edges, 4 thickened lines and two globular swellings on the claw.

7,000′. VIII.

G. Dyeriana, King and Pantling.

DIDYMOPLEXIS, Griffith.

Root with a chain of spindle-shaped tubers; stem erect, 7—15 cm. long, 3—4 mm. thick above its base, thinner upwards, and bearing 4—8 flowers at its upper end; flowers ochraceous-white tinged with brown; pedicels at first a few millimetres long, in fruit attaining a length of 12—15 cm.; sepals and petals cohering below into a tube and forming higher up two lips; the lip proper clawed, wedge-shaped truncate, median band with minute granules.

Bottom of tropical valleys; also Bengal, Assam, South India and Perak; probably parasitic on the roots of bamboos. V, VI.

D. pellens, Griffith.

APHYLLORCHIS, Blume.

1. Flowering plant 15—30 cm. high; stem 5 mm. and less thick; flowers 3—5 mm. across **2**

— Flowering plant 45—90 cm. high; lower part of stem 6—10 mm. thick; flowers 15 mm. and more across **3**

2. Upper part of stem and the floral axis pubescent; floral bracts longer than the ovary, linear, acuminate; sepals oblong, obtuse.

Lachen and Zemu valleys.

A. Pantlingii, W. W. Smith.

— Whole plant glabrous; bracts shorter than the untwisted ovary, lanceolate; sepals linear, acuminate.

Lachung valley, 10,000′. VII.

A. parviflora, King and Pantling.

3. Lower part of stem emitting thick roots; flowers like the whole plant pale-brown, 15—18 mm. across, each supported by a spreading bract, at first spreading, afterwards deflexed; dorsal sepal concave, overhanging the column; lip longer than the sepals, side-lobes narrow, end-lobe

bowl-shaped, upper surface beset with tubercles.

Guru Bathan, 2,000′; also Khasia (?) and Ceylon. VIII. **A. montana,** Reichenbach fil

— Rhizome long, clothed with small imbricating scales; flowers yellowish-red, 18—25 mm. across, each supported by a linear, 25—30 mm. long deflexed bract, ascending; sepals recurved; lip shorter than the petals with a winged claw, side-lobes erect, end-lobe trowel-shaped with an elliptical convexity at the tip.

Singa-li-la and Mon Lepcha, 13—14,000′. VII, VIII. **A. alpina,** King and Pantling.

GALEOLA, Lourier.

1. Extensive climbers, much branched, emitting roots; flowers no more than 25 mm. across **2**

— Stem erect, only the inflorescence branched; flowers 35 mm. and more in diameter **3**

2. Flowers in panicles; sepals all linear-oblong, recurved; lip deeply spoon-shaped, sides strongly incurved, bowl laciniate, upper surface papillose, basal part striped red; ripe capsule cylindric, 15—20 cm. long.

Rungit valley, 1,500′. VI.

G. Cathcartii, Hooker fil.

— Flowers in racemes, bell-shaped; dorsal sepal oblong, lateral ones obliquely ovate; lip bowl-shaped, edges erose, upper surface papillose-pubescent, base with red markings; ripe capsule cylindric, 20—24 cm. long.

Rishap valley. VII.

G. Hydra, Reichenbach fil.

3. Rhizome 3—6 cm. thick, clothed with large fleshy triangular scales; stem 150—250 cm. in height, flexuous, 2.5—3.5 cm. thick near its base; panicle 60—90 cm. long, its branches drooping, 7—24 cm. long; lip sessile, bowl-shaped with a short recurved spout, upper surface papillose except a central bare patch; flowers having an odour of vanilla; capsule with 3 sharp ridges, about 24 cm. long.

5—7,000′, not common; also westwards to Garhwal. VII, VIII.

G. Falconeri, Hooker fil.

— Rhizome 2.5 cm. thick, reddish, clothed in large fleshy cordate scales; stem 120—150 cm. high, straight, brownish purple, 1—1.5 cm. in thickness lower down; panicle with short, drooping, few-flowered branches; lip cup-shaped, with a very narrow 3-lobed border, upper surface entirely covered with papillæ, with two red patches; capsule obtusely triangular in cross-section, 15—18 cm. long.

5—7,000′; also Naga Hills.

G. Lindleyana, Reichenbach fil.

POGONIA, Jussieu.

1. Leaf and flower from the same bulb, contemporaneous; stem 5 cm. long; leaf reniform, nearly orbicular; petiole nearly 5 cm. long; flowers 2, about 25 mm. long; lip with two blunt triangular side-lobes and an ovate-oblong end-lobe and three basal ridges.

   3,000'. exceedingly rare. VIII.

   P. Hookeriana, King and Pantling.

— Leaf appearing after flowering on a different tuber **2**

2. Flowers 7 and more forming a raceme; tubers about 3 cm. in diameter; scape together with the raceme 20 cm. and more in length, about 5—6 mm. thick near the base; leaf 12—20 cm. broad **3**

   Flowers solitary or 2—3; tuber 6—18 mm. in diameter; scape 15 cm. and less in height, 3 mm. and less in thickness; leaf 10 cm. and less broad **4**

3. Scape 20—40 cm. long; raceme with 12 and more drooping flowers; flowers 16—18 mm. long; sepals and petals linear-lanceolate, green with dark-red lines; lip with green red-striated side-lobes. end-lobe broad-ovate, lavender-coloured with irregular red marks.

   Tropical valleys. 2,500'; also Chittagong. V. **P. Scottii**, Reichenbach fil.

— Scape 15—20 cm. long; raceme with 7 or 8 drooping flowers; flowers about 25 mm. long; sepals and petals broadly lanceolate, pink with white and dark-pink lines; lip pale green on the upper and white on the lower half.

2,000—2,500′; also Garhwal. V.

P. Gammieana, Hooker fil.

4. Flowers single 5

— Flowers 2 or 3; sepals and petals spreading, green; lip convolute with oblique opening, middle part of midrib forming a linear swelling with a yellow line, the lip otherwise lilac with a green basal spot; leaf dark green, mottled purplish-brown.

Near foot of hills, at Sembri, 1,500′. V.

P. plicata, Lindley.

5. Tubers 1.2—2 cm. in diameter; scape 7.5 —15 cm. long, greatest thickness about 3 mm.; flowers, including the ovary, about 3 cm. long 6

Tubers 6—9 mm. in diameter; scape 4—6.5 cm. long, about 1 mm. thick; flowers, including the ovary, 1—1.5 cm. long; sepals and petals linear, slightly diverging; lip with two short falcate side-lobes, a broad-obovate end-lobe and thickened glandular pubescent median line.

Western Bhotan Duars, east of Jaldacca river; probably rare; leaf not known. IV.

P. falcata, King and Pantling.

6. Leaf-stalk about 7.5 cm. long; sepals and petals oblong-linear or linear-oblanceolate, spreading, pale-green; lip slender-obconical with a semicircular fringed pink end-lobe.

Lachung valley, 6,500′. VI.

P. Prainiana, King and Pantling.

Leaf-stalk about 7.5 cm. long; sepals and petals linear-lanceolate, moderately divergent, white streaked with rose-colour; lip with a long convolute basal part and a concave elliptic-oblong, subacute end-lobe marked with rose-coloured spots and streaks.

Tropical valleys, ascending to 4,000′. IV.

P. macroglossa, Hooker fil.

CORYSANTHES, R. Brown.

Plant 5—7 cm. high; tuber depressed-globose, hairy; stem about 2 mm. thick; leaf at the upper end of the stem, cordate, ovate, acute, 8—13 mm. long, green with thick, white midrib and nerves; flower solitary, 15 mm. long; dorsal sepal oblanceolate, concave, arching over the column; lateral sepals filiform, forked; petals none; lip oblong, deflexed from the middle, basal part convolute, with two basal, cylindric straight spurs; lip and dorsal sepal transparent with purple markings.

Lachen valley, at Lamteng, 9,000′, on moist vertical rocks. VII.

C. himalaica, King and Pantling.

CEPHALANTHERA, Richard.

Rootstock horizontal; stem erect, 15—45 cm. long; leaves alternate, in two rows, 5—10 cm. long, 1—3 cm. broad, lanceolate, conduplicate; inflorescence terminal, racemose, 8—20-flowered; flowers 10—15 mm. long, white; sepals, petals and lip nearly upright; lip with a few yellow markings, lower part convolute, apical part concave, with 3—4 ribs.

Gnatong, 12,000′; also Kashmir to Bhotan. VII, VIII. **C. ensifolia,** Richard.

EPIPACTIS, Adamson.

1. Leaves broadly elliptic, lower ones 3.5—6.5 cm. long, 2.5—4 cm. broad; raceme rather dense, sometimes twisted; flowers about 13 mm. across, green; sepals broad-lanceolate, similar to each other, glabrous; basal part of lip bowl-shaped, apical part orbicular-ovate with two globular swellings at its base.

Gnatong, 11,000′; also westwards to Kashmir., VII. **E. latifolia,** Allioni.

— Leaves lanceolate, 15—20 cm. long, lowest between 3 and 4 cm. broad at their base, upper gradually narrower; raceme lax; flowers 18—25 mm. across; sepals and petals deep-lavender-coloured outside and there covered with white hairs, inside green with brown bands; dorsal sepal lanceolate, lateral ones twice as wide; basal part of lip trough-shaped, tubercled inside, purple, apical part lanceolate with erect side-lobes, pale-brown, with a white tip.

Tista valley on damp ground, 1,000′; also from Nipal to Peshawar. II, III.

E. consimilis, Wallich.

CORYMBIS, Thouars.

Root fibrous; stem 90—120 cm. high, stout; leaves elliptic-lanceolate, plaited, on a long ridged sheath, blade 30—45 cm. long; 7—10 cm. broad; panicles axillary, few-flowered, 7—10 cm. long; flowers white and fragrant; sepals and petals narrowly oblanceolate, 3—4 cm. long, at first cohering into a tube, finally free and spreading; lip with a long, linear claw, apical lobe orbicular, pointed, concave, less than half as long as the claw.

1,500—2,500′, in swampy ground; also Assam, Burma, Andamans and Nicobars.

C. veratrifolia, Reichenbach fil.

TROPIDIA, Lindley.

1. Stem 20—30 cm. high; 3—3.5 mm. thick near the base; leaves two, at the upper end of the stem, broad-elliptic, plaited, 10—13 cm. long, 5—8 cm. broad; spike terminal, conical, many-flowered, with its

peduncle rather shorter than the leaves; flowers crowded, about 16 mm. long; white flushed with pale ochre-colour; lateral sepals connate; lip broadly oblanceolate, with a basal cylindric, blunt spur.

Tista valley, 1,000—2,000′; also Assam, Burma, Malabar and Travancore. IX, X.

T. angulosa, Blume.

— Stem 30—60 cm. high, about 5 mm. thick near its base, sometimes branched; leaves more than six, scattered, elliptic-lanceolate, plaited, 9—15 cm. long, 16—30 mm. broad; inflorescence few-flowered, not exceeding 18 mm., terminal and leaf-opposed; flowers about 9 mm. long, white faintly tinged with yellow; sepals free, somewhat connivent; lip concave, narrow-oblong, bigibbous at the base.

Sembri, 1,000′; also Assam and Burma. XI.

T. curculioides, Lindley.

HERPYSMA, Lindley.

Stem decumbent and rooting below, then erect, 22—38 cm. long, 5—8 mm. thick; leaves scattered, elliptic-oblong or ovate-lanceolate, stalked, 5—9 cm. long, 18—38 mm. broad; raceme terminal, 25—30 mm. long, hairy; flowers about 13 mm. long; dorsal sepal and petals forming a hood, white with the upper part of the midrib orange or pink, lateral sepals white tipped pink or orange; lip with two erect, denticulate basal lobes and a subquadrate, bluntly apiculate end-lobe.

Above Sureil, 3—5,000′; also Nipal and Khasia VIII, IX. **H. longicaulis,** Lindley.

PHYSURUS, Richard.

Stem decumbent and rooting at the base, then erect, with the inflorescence 20—25 cm. high, 6 mm. thick at the base; leaves 3—4, obliquely ovate, stalked, 5—7-nerved, 6—10 cm. long; 30—38 mm. broad; peduncle long; raceme 4—5 cm. long; flowers from tip of dorsal sepal to tip of spur about 18 mm. long; sepals and petals pale-reddish-brown, lip white, oblong, terminal lobe small and deflexed, side-lobes erect; spur irregularly cylindric, with a bifid tip.

British Bhotan, above Engo, 5,000′. IV.
Ph. herpysmoides, King and Pantling.

SPIRANTHES, Richard.

Root tuberous; whole plant 15—45 cm. high; leaves close-set near the base, linear, 19—60 mm. long, 6 mm. and less broad; spike 8—15 cm. long; axis pubescent; flowers along a spiral, crowded, 2.5—5 mm. long; white or pink; sepals ovate-oblong, petals linear, tips of both reflexed; lip oblong, the apical part nearly quadrate with a wavy margin.

2—8,000′, common; also hilly parts of the whole of India. VIII—IX.

Sp. australis, Lindley.

GOODYERA, R. Brown.

1. Leaves nearly uniformly green .. **2**

— Leaves green with white lines or darker green blotches **5**

2. Leaves inserted for some distance up the erect part of the stem; blade 7—25 cm. long **3**

— Leaves clustered close to the base of the upright part of the stem, blade 2.5—4 cm. long; raceme 7—8 cm. long, many-flowered; flowers close-set; sepals connivent, like the petals white; lip forming a subglobose, pinkish-yellow sack suddenly contracted into a decurved green beak.

Lachung valley, 12,000′; also Garhwal. VIII. **G. fusca,** Lindley.

3. The whole plant 25—80 cm. high; stem 8—10 mm. thick; flowers ascending, dull-red or white; end-lobe of lip small, ovate or triangular, not coiled up **4**

— The whole plant 70—100 cm. high; stem about 13 mm. thick; leaf-blade 15—25 cm. long; flowers at right-angles to the floral axis; lip pale-brown, interior of the pouch-like basal part bristly, end-lobe linear, revolute; sepals and petals spreading, pale green.

Rangbi, 6,000′, rare also Ceylon. III.
G. fumata, Thwaites.

4. Leaf-stalk about one-third to one-half the length of the blade, broadly sheathing; raceme very dense with very many (80 and more) flowers, 8—20 cm. long, narrow-cylindric; flowers 5 mm. across, sub-globose, white faintly tinged with green; sepals incurved, subequal; basal part of lip ovoid-saccate, the interior with two rows of teeth on the sides and a globular swelling at the end of the row; end-lobe triangular, decurved.

1,000—4,000′, common; also from Nipal to Bhotan, Assam, Khasia, South India and Ceylon. V. **G. procera,** Hooker.

— Leaf-stalk one-half to two-third of the length of the blade, narrow, expanding into a very short sheath; raceme somewhat lax, with 25—35 flowers, 10—13 cm. long, slender-conical in outline; flowers about 18 mm. across, dull-red; dorsal sepal ovate concave, lateral ovate-oblong, spreading, with recurved tips; lip globular-saccate, bristly within, end-lobe narrow-ovate, reflexed.

Tista valley, at Ramtek, 4,000.′ VIII.
G. grandis, King and Pantling.

5. At least the larger leaves 5 cm. and more long, not white-reticulate 6

Leaves 4.5 cm. long and less, green with a white net-work along nerves and veins **8**

6. Leaves pale-green mottled with darker green, uppermost not close to the raceme; peduncle about 10 cm. long, strict; floral bracts shorter than the flowers (including the ovary), like the floral axis and the ovaries densely glandular-pubescent; basal part of lip globular-saccate, bristly inside, apical part ovate, concave, with two thick lamellæ, lip white tipped with green, sepals and petals yellowish-pink.

   Labba, 6,000′; also Khasia and Manipur. IX—I. **G. secundiflora,** Griffith.

— Leaves green with white lines or a white median band, upper ones close to the raceme, peduncle no more than 5 cm. long

7. Leaves 2.5—5 cm. long, ovate-lanceolate, with a broad silvery band along the midrib, lower surface suffused with purple; axis of one-sided raceme glabrous or sparsely hairy; bracts lanceolate, not overtopping the pink, horizontal flowers; petals partially cohering; basal part of lip forming an ovoid sack bristly inside, apical part lanceolate, recurved, with two lamellæ.

   6—10,000′. VII—IX. **G. vittata,** Bentham.

— Leaves 6—9 cm. long, obliquely elliptic-oblong or oblong-lanceolate, 5-nerved, wavy, green with three silvery lines; axis of raceme, bracts and ovaries glandular-pubescent; flowers all-sided; bracts overtopping the flowers, linear; sepals connivent, pinkish or orange; petals free, pale-pink; basal part of lip globular, yellow, hispid inside, apical lobe triangular-oblong, slightly recurved, not lamellate, orange and white.

Mostly 5—6,000′, Senchal 7,000′; also Assam, Naga Hills and Khasia, Burma, Perak. X, XI. **G. foliosa,** Bentham.

8. Upright part of the stem about 5 mm. thick near the ground; leaves inserted along the stem; peduncle hardly any .. **9**

— Peduncle 2—3 mm. thick near its base, 7—15 cm. long; leaves crowded near the ground, ovate- or elliptic-oblong, 12—25 mm. long, 9—12 mm. broad, green, white-reticulated; flowers globular, white flushed with brownish-pink; basal part of lip ovoid-saccate, naked inside, apical part ovate, acute.

8—11,000′, common; also westward to Simla. VII, VIII. **G. repens,** Brown.

9. Axis of inflorescence, bracts and ovaries covered with long, thin, stiffish hairs; flowers numerous, ovoid, 4—5 mm. long; sepals olive-green, densely covered with minute glandular hairs; petals and lip dirty-white; basal part of lip globose-saccate, bristly inside, apical part triangular-oblong.

Tista valley, at Kalijhora, 1,000′; also Khasia. IX. **G. hispida,** Lindley.

— Peduncle and raceme pubescent: flowers about 10, ovoid-oblong, about 10 mm. long, white; sepals white, tipped with pink, laxly hairy; basal part of lip bowl-shaped with a sharp tooth on each side of its mouth, bristly inside, apical part broadly linear, obtuse, recurved at the tip.

Senchal, 7,000′. VII.

G. Hemsleyana, King and Pantling.

ZEUXINE, Lindley.

1. Lower part of sepals coherent into a tube; flowering stem bare or nearly so; flowers 1—4, 6—9 mm. long, pure white .. **2**

— Sepals entirely free; flowering stem mostly with leaves; flowers rarely as few as 3, usually more than 4 .. .. **3**

2. Basal part of lip ovoid-saccate; apical part abruptly deflexed, deeply divided into two divergent linear lobules.

Above Sureil, 6,500′. VIII.

Z. Franchetiana, King and Pantling.

— Basal part of lip forming a wide shallow sack with 2 large swellings inside, the sack contracting into a long convolute claw terminated by two obovate, obliquely truncate diverging lobules.

Tendong, 6,000′. VII.

Z. pumila, King and Pantling.

3. Apical part of lip divided into two lobules **4**

— Apical part of lip undivided **10**

4. Leaves membranous, ovate-oblong or ovate-lanceolate; flowers usually more than three; sepals and petals connivent .. **5**

— Leaves leathery, broadly ovate, blackish-purple on the upper surface with a white midrib, crowded near the base of the upright part of the stem; flowers 2—3; sepals and petals spreading, pale-brown; basal part of lip boat-shaped, yellow with two swellings inside the sack, apical part divided into two divergent subquadrate white lobules.

Lachung valley, 7,500′. VIII.

Z. pulchra, King and Pantling.

5. Leaves fresh, not withered at flowering time **6**

— Leaves withered at flowering time .. **9**

6. Leaves clustered near the base of the peduncle **7**

— Leaves scattered . .. **8**

7. Leaves lanceolate-ovate, 2.5—6.5 cm. long, 16—25 mm. broad, green suffused with grey or with a broad grey median stripe; floral axis with short spreading hairs; lateral sepals widely spreading; sepals green; petals white; lip longer than the

sepals, basal part boat-shaped, middle part convolute, apical part with two spreading, quadrate yellow lobules.

2,000′; also Bhotan and Assam. IV.
Z. nervosa, Bentham.

— Leaves lanceolate, 2.5—3.8 cm. long, 6—9 mm. broad, blackish-purple, floral axis densely glandular-pubescent; sepals connivent, like the petals and most parts of the lip olive-green; lip about as long as the sepals, basal part widely saccate, middle part curved inwards and white, apical part with two recurved obliquely ovate, blunt lobules.

Bhotan Duars, 2,000′. III.
Z. glandulosa, King and Pantling.

8. Leaves long-petioled; flowers about 10, about half as long as the glabrous ovary and the bract, sepals pale-brown; petals white; basal part of lip pale-yellow, apical part white, tapering to the decurved bilobulate tip, lobules obliquely ovate, subacute.

Bhotan, at Ambiok, 4,000′; also Khasia. IX. **Z. abbreviata,** Hooker fil.

— Leaves very short-petioled; flowers about 20, about as long as the pubescent bract and ovary; sepals green; petals whitish-green; lip yellow, apical lobe with two recurved divergent truncate lobules.

Rangit valley, 1,500′; also Bhotan, Khasia, Tenasserim and Penang. IV.
Z. affinis, Bentham.

9. Leaves scattered; flowers 6 mm. long; sepals nearly equal, green; petals lanceolate, white; basal part of lip saccate, white; apical part with two rectangularly oblong yellow lobules.

Mangpu, 3,500′. IV.

Z. reflexa, King and Pantling.

— Leaves clustered close to the base of the peduncle; flowers about 12 mm. long; sepals unequal, dull greyish-olive, dorsal larger, very concave; petals oblong-elliptic, white; lip boat-shaped, basal part dull-pink, apical part with two nearly square obliquely diverging yellow lobules.

From the foot of the hills up to 3,000′; also Nipal, Assam, Tenasserim, Ceylón. V, VI. **Z. flava,** Bentham.

10. Leaves 2—4, close to the base of the peduncle, ovate, 25—30 mm. long, 16—19 mm. broad, velvety green with a pure white stripe abong the midrib; raceme lax; flowers about 10, 6 mm. long, pink into white; dorsal sepals ovate, lateral sepals lanceolate, often green; lip saccate, ending in a small terminal lobe.

6,000′; also Assam and Burma. IX, X.

Z. goodyeroides, Lindley.

— Leaves all along the erect part of the stem, linear, acuminate, green, the larger ones about 3 cm. long and 5 mm. broad; raceme dense; flowers 20 and more, white or pink; dorsal sepal ovate, lateral falcate; basal part of lip purple, shallowly boat-shaped with two triangular teeth inside; apical lobe rhombic, yellow; petals united to the dorsal sepal into a hood.

Foot of hills; also all over India in grassy places. I. **Z. sulcata,** Lindley.

ANOECTOCHILUS, Blume.

1. Leaves of various tints of red or brown .. 2

— Leaves either uniformly green or green marked with white lines 4

2. Leaves either uniformly brown or olive-green above and coppery below; flowers 2—3, 25 mm. long; sepals green with white midrib and brown tips; petals falcate, white (or green); lip white, basal part forming a globose, shortly bifid, green sack with two shortly conical teeth inside; claw with six coarse brown teeth on each side; apical lobe ending in two diverging, obliquely oblong or nearly quadrate lobules.

Chungtang and other places, 3,000—6,000′; also Shillong and Kohima. VII, VIII.
A. Elwesii, King and Pantling.

— Leaves purplish-red with golden reticulations 3

4. Lip uppermost, pure white, spurred; spur conical, tip minutely bilobed, as long as the lateral sepals, with two warty processes inside; claw with 7 or 8 slender teeth on

either side forming two fringes; apical lobe divided into two linear, blunt, spreading, recurved lobules; leaves having a velvety lustre, the mid-area red passing into golden or greenish-yellow tinged with pink.

Bottom of tropical valleys and foot of hills; also Kalka to Manipur.

A. Roxburghii, Lindley.

— Lip below white, spurred; spur green, pouch-like, short, bifid, with two ovoid swellings inside; claw with four small green teeth on either side; apical lobe divided into two divergent, obliquely wedge-shaped lobules; leaves with a velvety sheen, very dark-red above with golden veins and dull-red below.

3—5,000′, fairly common. **IX.**

A. sikkimensis, King and Pantling.

4. Flowers 10 and more; upright part of plant 22—45 cm. high **5**

— Flowers 3—8; upright part of plant 10—20 cm. high **6**

5. Stem about 5 mm. thick below; leaves ovate to ovate-lanceolate, 3—6 cm. long, 1—3 cm. broad, green with three white nerves; sepals and petals pale green, the dorsal sepal tinged with brown; lip brilliant yellow, basal part forming a globose sack with two spur-like processes within; claw with 7 or 8 oblique, unequal, coarse awl-shaped teeth on either side;

apical lobe with two diverging, obliquely truncate lobules.

5—6,000′ ; Yoksum at 7,000′ ; also Khasia. VII—IX. **A. lanceolatus,** Lindley.

— Stem 8—11 mm. thick below; leaves elliptic, 5—7-nerved, green, 6—9 cm. long, 36—50 mm. broad; sepals and petals pale-green mottled white and tipped with pink; lip white, basal part flushed yellow, forming an oblong pouch; claw narrow-cylindric with about 5 very unequal awl-shaped green teeth on either side; apical lobe divided into two divergent linear-oblong, obliquely truncate lobules.

4—6,000′; Tendong; also Khasia. VII. **A. grandiflorus,** Lindley.

6. Stem 6—7 mm. thick near the ground; leaves elliptic to ovate-lanceolate, about 5 cm. long and 18—25 mm. broad; sepals and petals green; dorsal sepal broad-ovate, forming with the petals a hood over the column; lip white, basal part forming a subglobose sak; claw with 8—9 very unequal teeth on either side, apical lobe twisted, divided into two slightly divergent obtriangular lobules.

Bhotan, 4,000′. XII. **A. tortus.** King and Pantling.

— Stem 3 mm. thick near the ground; leaves ovate, 12—18 mm. long; sepals green, petals and lip white; dorsal sepal with recurved tip; lip with a small globular sack at the base, a long, narrow, untoothed claw and an apical lobe divided half-way down into two broad, truncate lobules.

Mahalderam Peak, 6,000′; also Khasia. IX.

A. crispus, Lindley.

CHEIROSTYLIS, Blume.

Stem decumbent at the base, upright part of plant 10—18 cm., 5 mm. thick near the ground; leaves ovate, 18—25 mm. long, withered at flowering time: flowers 1—2, pure white, 18 mm. long; base of lip shallowly boat-shaped, middle part forming a long, narow claw, end-lobe circular when flattened out, fringed with a number of linear, obtuse teeth.

Bhotan, 4,000′, near the Jaldacca river; also Khasia and Burma. XII.

Ch. Griffithii, Lindley.

HETAERIA, Blume.

Upright part of stem 25—45 cm. high, 6 mm. thick near the base; leaves ovate to elliptic, 7—13 cm. long, 4—5 cm. broad, 5-nerved; raceme 7—10 cm. long; flowers 20 or more, on an erect ovary, themselves slightly inclined downwards, about 9 mm. long; sepals and petals green, tipped with pink; lip short, nearly hemisphæric green, with a very small, white, apical lobe.

1,500—4,000′, very common; also Chittagong, Assam, and Burma. I, II.

H. rubens, Bentham.

ORCHIS, Linnaeus.

1. Rhizome thin, not tuberous; upright part of plant 5—20 cm. high; leaf solitary, more rarely a smaller one higher up; lower leaf elliptic-oblong, blunt, tapering into a petiole; peduncle slender, about 2 mm. thick; flowers 1—4, about 12 mm. from tip of dorsal sepal to tip of lip, white or purple; lip broad-elliptic, with numeral shallow longitudinal grooves, as long as the sepals; spur nearly cylindric, about half as long as the ovary.

   Singa-le-la range, 12,000′; Gnatong 11,000′; Lachung valley; Chumbi; also Garhwal. VII.

   O. spathulata, Reichenbach fil.

— Roots tuberous; leaves lanceolate or linea. 2

2. Height of whole plant 30—50 cm.; tuber digitate; leaves elliptic-lanceolate, 5—13 cm. long, 18—30 mm. broad; spike dense, narrow-cylindric, many-flowered; flowers of pink or violet tints, rarely white, 6 mm. across; lip broadly oblong, with a shallow middle lobe; spur subcylindric, slightly club-shaped, as long as the ovary.

   Singa-le-la range and Lachung valley, 12,000′; Chumbi valley; also Nipal and Western Himalaya. VIII.

   O. habenarioides, King and Pantling.

— Height of flowering plant 5—25 cm.; tuber small, entire; leaves lanceolate-linear to linear, not more than 10 mm. broad; flowers less than 10; end-lobe of lip 2—3-lobulate 3

3. Flowering plant 10—25 cm. high; leaves linear-lanceolate, 3.6—7.5 cm. long, 5—8 mm. broad; flowers dark-purple, 4 or more; lip with 3 equal oblong lobes rounded at their tips, the lateral divergent; spur cylindric, slightly club-shaped, as long as the ovary.

Singa-le-la range, Lachung valley and elsewhere at 10—13,000′; also Nipal and Kumaon. VII, VIII. **O. Chusua,** Don.

— Flowering plant not exceeding 8 cm. in height; leaves less than 4 mm. broad; flowers 1 or 2 4

4. Flowers dark-purple; lateral sepals recurved; lip broadly trapezoidal, shortly and unequally three-lobed; spur slender conical, blunt, as long as the ovary.

Sikkim, 10—13,000′. VII, VIII.
O. Chusua, Don,
var. **nana,** King and Pantling.

— Flowers white; sepals concave, connivent; lip three-lobed, end-lobe again two-lobed, lateral lobes and apical lobules shortly oblong, truncate, of nearly equal size; spur half as long as the ovary.

Lachung valley, 10,000′. VII.
O. puberula, King and Pantling

HABENARIA, Willdenow.

1. Lip entire, not three-lobed or three-partite, sometimes with two auricles or two minute teeth at or near its base .. **2**

— Lip variously three-lobed or three partite **14**

2. Spur shorter than the ovary **3**

— Spur longer than the ovary or about as long as the ovary **7**

3. Stem 2—3 mm. thick near its base, one- or two-leaved .. .. ..

— Stem 5—8 mm. thick, with 3—5 leaves .. **6**

4. Flowers inserted on the upper side of the recurved floral axis, with the ovary about 8 mm. long, white; lip linear-oblong, recurved, tapering towards the thicker tip; spur shortly spindle-shaped, shorter than the sepals; leaf narrowly elliptic-oblong, 3—6 cm. long; tubers cylindric.

Yak-la, 10,000′; Nipal frontier, 12,000′; Cho-la, Chumbi; Ti-am-phung and Re-chi-la 9,000′. **H. urceolata,** Clarke.

— Flowers inserted all round the straight floral axis; lip ovate oblong, tapering to the blunt tip; spur short cylindric. .. **5**

5. Flowers somewhat remote from each other; lip situated below the other parts of

the flower, ovary twisted through half a turn; spur somewhat compressed.

Lachen and Lachung valleys; Gnatong and Singa-le-la, 11—12,000′. VIII.

H. juncea, King and Pantling

— Flowers close-set, white; lip above the other parts of the flower, the ovary being spirally twisted through a complete turn; spur slightly recurved.

Re-chi-la, 9,000′; Ling-tu and near Gantok, 10,000′. VIII.

H. nematocaulon, Hooker fil.

6. Stem 22—40 cm. high; leaves lanceolate 5—8 cm. long; flowers about 20, spike about 10 cm. long; sepals cohering and with the petals forming a kind of hood; lip fleshy, much decurved, linear-oblong, with two minute teeth near its base; spur cylindric, blunt, slightly club-shaped.

Senchal, 8,000′; Singa-le-la, 10,000′. VII.

H. Biermanniana, King and Pantling.

— Stem 30—75 cm. high; leaves narrow-elliptic, 6—10 cm. long; flowers green, 40 or more; spike 15 15 cm. long; dorsal sepal erect, lateral spreading; lip linear, with a transverse swelling near its base; spur markedly clavate, laterally compressed inserted with a very narrow base.

Singa-le-la range and Lachung valley, 8—12,000′; also from Chumbi to Simla. VII, VIII.

H. densa, Wallich.

7. Spur twice or less than twice as long as the lip **8**

— Spur three or four times as long as the lip; dorsal sepal and petals connivent into a hood **13**

8. Stem, including the sheath, 8—10 mm. thick near its base; leaves usually inserted close to each other, 3—5, sometimes only 2, unequal in size, the larger ones 4—7 cm. broad; flowers 12 to more than 20 .. **9**

— Stem, including the sheath, 5 mm. or less in thickness near its base; leaves scattered or single, the large ones 1.5—3.5 cm. in breadth; flowers 12 or less, green .. **11**

9. Without tuber, but with thick, fleshy roots; flowering plant 30—60 cm. high; leaves 3—4 gradually attenuated into a long sheath, the lowest usually the largest, oblong-oblanceolate, up to 25 cm. long; spike 12—24 cm. long, lax; distance between the lower flowers 20—15 mm.; flowers about at right-angles to the floral axis, from the base of the ovary to the tip of the lip about 3 cm.; sepals and petals green, dorsal sepal and petals erect, lateral sepals spreading; lip yellowish, lanceolate, three-nerved; spur slender, cylindric, slightly wider towards the tip.

8—12,000′; also Chumbi valley. VII—IX.
H. stenantha, Hooker fil.

— Root tuberous; distance between the flowers 5 mm. and less; flowers ascending **10**

10. Tubers stoutly spindle-shaped; flowering plant 20—45 cm. high; leaves about 5, the middle ones 5—10 cm. long, ovate or elliptic-oblong; spike 7—25 cm. long, moderately dense, narrow-cylindric; flowers often more than 20, about 15 mm. from tip of the broad, concave, erect dorsal sepal to the tip of the lip; petals spreading, lanceolate or linear, like the lip greenish-yellow; lip with recurved edges, longer than the sepals.

Lachen and Lachung valleys; Singa-le-la range, 8—10,000′, common; westward to Kashmir. VII—IX.

H. latilabris, Hooker fil.

— Tubers short-cylindric; flowering plant 15—25 cm. high; leaves 2—4, broad-elliptic to elliptic-lanceolate, 5—8 cm. long; spike 3—8 cm. long, dense, stoutly cylindric; flowers about 15, about 20 mm. from the tip of the ovate, erect sepal to tip of the fleshy, subcylindric, abruptly deflexed lip, uniformly green; petals fleshy, erect, triangular, lip longer than the sepals.

Lachung valley; Gnatong, 11,000′. VII.

H. Cumminsiana, King and Pantling.

11. Stem about 4 mm. thick near the base; leaves 1 or 2; lip inclined obliquely downwards 12

— Stem 2—3 mm. thick near its base; leaves 3—4, scattered, 25—38 mm. long, oblong-lanceolate; lip deflexed, fleshy, narrow-triangular, with two basal auricles and an abruptly bent tip; dorsal sepal and petals erect, lanceolate, lateral sepals narrowly oblong, reflexed; spike lax, very slender; bracts ovate-oblong; spur slender-conical.

Lachen valley, 11,000′. VIII.
H. Dyeriana, King and Pantling.

12. Leaves (usually 2) lanceolate, 6—10 cm. long; raceme lax, distance between the lower flowers about 2 cm.; bracts foliaceous, linear, 12—65 mm. long, the lower ones much longer than the ovary and curled back; dorsal sepal triangular, lateral ones lanceolate, revolute; petals falcate, acuminate; lip membranous, ovate at the base, and caudate upwards; spur narrow-cylindric, incurved.

Senchal, 8,000′; Singa-le-la and Lachung valley, 12,000′; Ling-tu and Ze-lap-la. VIII, IX. **H. sikkimensis,** Hooker fil.

— Leaf usually solitary, broadly oblanceolate, 2.5—12 cm. long; raceme rather dense, distance between the flowers 1 cm. and less; bracts linear-lanceolate, the lower ones 2.5—3 cm. long, somewhat incurved; dorsal sepal and petals obliquely ovate, erect, connivent into a hood, lateral sepals reflexed; lip ovate-lanceolate, shorter than the cylindric and slightly club-shaped spur.

Lachen valley, 10—12,000′; Jengri, Nalong and Na-tut. VII—IX.
H. oligantha, Hooker fil.

13. Stem about 3 mm. thick near its base; leaves 2, remote, lower elliptic-lanceolate, 5—13 cm. long, 18 mm. and less broad, the upper about half as long, narrow-lanceolate, broadest near its base; raceme narrow, lax, about 6-flowered, 2.5—7.5 cm. long; the fleshy lip oblong-lanceolate, deflexed and curved inwards.

Lachung valley, 9—11,000′. VII—IX.

H. leptocaulon, Hooker fil.

Stem 5—6 mm. thick near its base; leaves more than two, scattered, lowest oblong 10—13 cm. long, about one-third as broad, upper lanceolate, gradually smaller; raceme 10—18 cm. long, very lax; the fleshy lip ovate-oblong, about at right-angles to the plane of the hood.

Lachen valley, 9,000′; Singa-le-la range, 10—12,000′. VII.

H. Bakeriana, King and Pantling.

14. Side-lobes of lip obliquely cuneate, oblong or lanceolate **15**

— Side-lobes of lip linear or awl-shaped, or divided into filiform segments, or sepals, petals and divisions of the lip prolonged into filiform appendices **24**

15. Leaf or leaves lanceolate or linear, 5—20 times as long as broad **16**

— Leaves ovate, elliptical or oblong, 2—4 times as long as broad **17**

16. Leaves linear, 2—3, 5—13 mm. broad; flowers rather crowded, inserted on one side of the floral axis, pink; sepals and petals connivent to form together a hood over the column; lip three-lobed, the oblong middle lobe somewhat longer than the triangular side-lobes; spur shorter than the sepals, funnel-shaped.

Lachung valley, 9—11,000′; also Chumbi valley and Kumaon. VIII, IX.

H. secundiflora, Hooker fil.

— Leaf usually solitary, oblong-lanceolate, 12—20 mm. broad; flowers rather remote, green; only the dorsal sepal together with the petals connivent to form a hood; middle lobe of lip considerably longer than the side-lobes; spur pouch-shaped, much shorter than the sepals.

10—12,000′; Lachen and Lachung valleys and at Gnatong; also N. W. Himalaya.

H. fallax, King and Pantling

17. Distance between tip of dorsal sepal and tip of lip 20—30 mm. **18**

— Distance between tip of dorsal sepal and tip of lip 3—8 mm. **19**

18. Stem about 6—8 mm. thick near its base; flowering plant 30—75 cm. high; leaves one above the other, not forming a whorl, elliptic-oblong; spike 5—10 cm. long, rather lax; flowers less than 10, white; lip with two wedge-shaped or rounded side-lobes and a much shorter oblong end-lobe;

spur either absent or longer than the ovary, funnel-shaped at the base, very slender club-shaped towards the tip, bent knee-shape between the two parts.

2,500—5,000′, common; also trom Nipal to Burma. **H. geniculata,** Don.

— Stem about 1 cm. thick near its base; flowering plant 50—75 cm. high; leaves 5—6 in a whorl at the base of the peduncle, elliptic; spike 12—24 cm. long, cylindric, dense; flowers very many; sepals pale-brown, petals and lip white; side-lobes of lip narrow-lanceolate, falcate, apical part bent outwards; mid-lobe about half the length of the side-lobes, narrow-triangular, blunt; spur subglobular, small, green.

Valley of the Tista and elsewhere, 1,500′; also Assam and Chittagong Hills to Burma. VI, VII.
H. constricta, Hooker fil

19. Tuber depressed-globular; flowering plant 20 cm. and less in height; leaves 2, alternate, broad-elliptic to elliptic-oblong, 25—38 mm. long; spike 8—10-flowered. 25—38 mm. long; sepals green, petals and lip white; lip tripartite, segments parallel, lateral ones shorter; spur nearly cylindric, horizontal.

Jongri. 13,000′. VI.
H. albomarginata, King and Pantling.

— Tuber ellipsoid or oblong; flowering plant, 30—75 cm. high; leaves 3—5; spike more than 10-flowered, 4 and more cm. long; spur globular or widely fusiform .. **20**

20. Stem about 8 mm. thick near its base; whole plant 30—45 cm. high; leaves 4—5, forming a whorl at the base of the peduncle, ovate or elliptic, 6--13 cm. long; spike 10—20 cm. long, narrow; sepals brown, tinged olive, petals and lip olive-green; lip curved in the shape of an S; end-lobe ovate-oblong, side-lobes shorter; spur obovoid.

At Silake, 2,000′; also Burma and Andamans. VI.

H. Parishii, Reichenbach fil.

— Stem 7 mm. and less near its base; leaves not forming a whorl; spur globular .. **21**

21. Spike 10 mm. or less across at its widest; flowers about 4 mm. wide, brownish-green; side-lobes of lip shorter than the midlobe, pointing forwards **22**

— Spike 15 mm. or more across at its widest; flowers about 8 mm. wide, white or cream-coloured, sometimes somewhat greenish; side-lobes of lip slightly longer than the midlobe, diverging **23**

22. Whole plant 45—70 cm. high; leaves remote from each other, elliptic-oblong; lip equalling the sepals in length.
Chung-thang, 5,500′. VII.

H. pseudophrys, King and Pantling.

— Whole plant 30—45 cm. high; leaves crowded about the middle, ovate-oblong, lip somewhat longer than the sepals.

Mangpu, 3,500′; also Assam to Burma. VIII. **H. Prainii,** Hooker fil.

23. Stem 45—60 cm. high; spike with peduncle 25—30 cm. long; leaves rather crowded, the larger about 3.5 cm. broad; flowers sweet-scented.

Sivoke, 1,000′; Mangpu 3,000′; also Nipal to Manipur, and on Pareshnath. V—VII.
H. goodyeroides, Don.

— Stem 30—45 cm. high; spike with peduncle 12—15 cm. long; leaves somewhat remote, the larger about 2.5 cm. broad.

Western Sikkim. 2,000′; also Garhwal to Khasia. VI, VII.
H. goodyeroides, *var.* **affinis,** Don.

24. Side-lobes of lip deeply divided on the outer side into narrow-linear spreading segments staghorn fashion **25**

— Side-lobes of lip entire **26**

25. Leaves linear, gradually attenuated from base to tip, strongly three-nerved; raceme, 8—15 cm. long; flowers 3—4 cm. in diameter; dorsal sepal lanceolate, erect, forming a hood with the petals, the three greenish-white; lateral sepals erect, dark-green; lip white; spur somewhat longer than the ovary.

Namgah, 5,000′; also Khasia and westwards to Simla. VIII. **H. pectinata,** Don.

— Leaves ovate-oblong, acute or acuminate, strongly five-nerved; raceme 12—20 cm. long; flowers about 4 cm. across, green throughout; lateral sepals broad-lanceolate, spreading; spur much longer than the ovary.

Tumlong and Re-chi-la, 6—9,000′; also Khasia and westwards to Simla. VII, VIII. **H. arietina,** Hooker fil.

26. All parts of the flower with long, thread-like tails and pale-green; spike dense, but only 5—8 cm. long; petals consisting of two hair-like, flexuous segments.

5.000′. VIII, IX. **H. polytricha,** Hooker fil.

— At least the sepals and petals, mostly also the lip not tailed **27**

27. Middle segment of lip longer than or at least as long as the lateral segments .. **28**

— Middle segment of lip shorter than the lateral segments **29**

28. Leaves inserted on the second fourth part of the stem, .7—3 cm. long, narrow-elliptic; spike 10—25 cm. long, rather lax, its axis triangular in cross-section; ovary long-beaked; flowers pale-green, 15 mm. in diameter; dorsal sepal hooded, lateral reflexed; petals triangular, small; segments of lip thread-like, middle one

conspicuously flexuous; spur about half as long as the ovary, slender-conical, incurved.

Sikkim, 5—6,000′; also Khasia. VIII, IX.
H. malleifera, Hooker fil.

— Leaves inserted on the upper two-third of the stem, ovate- or oblong-lanceolate, 7—20 cm. long; spike 10—23 cm. long, dense; axis terete, flowers arranged in a close spiral; ovary not beaked; flowers about 25 mm. in diameter, sepals and petals pale-green, spreading or reflexed; petals produced downwards as a wing; lip brown, with two recurved lateral, and a usually longer fleshy awl-shaped, horizontally projecting middle segment; spur as long as the ovary, two-ridged, up-turned.

2—6,000′; also from Garhwal to Bengal and Assam. VIII—X.
H. stenopetala, Lindley.

29. Spur as long as, or longer than the ovary **30**

— Spur much shorter than the ovary .. **31**

30. Whole plant about 12 cm. high; leaves two, inserted about 2.5 cm. above the base, opposite, orbicular, about 3 cm. in diameter; peduncle glandular-pubescent; raceme 3.5—5 cm. long; flowers 4—6, greenish, about 18 mm. in diameter; dorsal sepal and petals forming a hood; lip divided to the base into three linear segments, the lateral ones with recurved tips;

spur as long as the ovary, curved forwards, clavate towards the apex.

Lachen valley, 10—11,000′; also westwards to Kashmir. VII.

H. Aitchisoni, Reichenbach fil.

— Whole plant 25—45 cm. high; leaves 5—6, crowded near the base of the slender peduncle, elliptic-oblong, 6—13 cm. long; raceme 12—18 cm. long, somewhat lax; flowers many, green, about 13 mm. in diameter; dorsal sepal and the equally long petals forming a hood; lip divided to the base into three segments, the lateral ones awl-shaped, slightly incurved from the ends of a short cross-piece, the middle segment stouter and blunt; spur longer than the ovary, awl-shaped, incurved.

Below Mim, 3,000′; also from Garhwal to Assam, Eastern Bengal and Orissa. VII, VIII. **H. furcifera,** Lindley.

31. Tubers oblong; the whole plant 30—50 cm. high; stem about 5 mm. thick near its base; leaves 3—5, inserted higher up, elliptic-lanceolate, 5—10 cm. long, 12—18 mm. broad; spike narrow, 5—20 cm. long, flowers about 12 mm. across, green: lip tripartite, lateral segments thread-like, nearly horizontal, slightly curved upwards, longer than the middle linear obtuse segment; spur shortly club-shaped or spindle-shaped.

Labba, Chungthang, Tumlong, Pashating, 6—7,000′; also Khasia and Ceylon.

H. aristata, Hooker fil.

Tuber obliquely ellipsoid; the whole plant 15—45 cm. high; stem about 2 mm. thick near its base; leaves 2 or 3, close together near the base of the stem, oblong, 5—10 cm. long, 12—30 mm. broad; spike very narrow, 3—15 cm. long, rather lax; flowers scarcely 4 mm. across, green; lip deflexed from the middle and there divided into three segments; lateral segment oblong, blunt, shorter.

Guru Bathan, (1,500′?); also from Khasia to Penang. VIII.

H. tentaculata, Reichenbach fil.

HERMINIUM, Linnaeus.

1. Stem about 2 mm. thick at its base; leaves not longer than 4 cm., usually one, more rarely two **2**

   Stem at least 3 mm. thick at the base; leaves mostly much longer than 4 cm., rarely only 3 cm. long, 2—4 .. .. **5**

2. Spike rather dense; flowers inserted on one side of the floral axis; lip very broadly ovate, nearly as broad as long; sepals oblong, obtuse, subequal, erect; petals broad-elliptic; spur very small, short-cylindric; leaves subopposite, broadly ovate and white-veined, or scattered oblanceolate, obtuse and uniformly green, sometimes obsolete.

Singa-le-la range, 12,000′; Chumbi valley; Lachung valley; also Nipal. VII.

H. orbiculare, Hooker fil.

— Spike lax; flowers spirally disposed; lip linear or narrowly triangular; spur absent; leaves solitary 3

3. Dorsal sepal and petals forming a hood over the column; lip triangular or in its anterior part awl-shaped 4

— Dorsal sepal and petals not forming a hood; lip linear, deflexed; leaf elliptic, 16—18 mm. long; dorsal sepal broadly ovate, concave, curved forwards; lateral sepals and petals nearly equal, narrow-oblong, the former deflexed

Singa-le-la and Lingtu, 11—12,000′. VII.

H. angustilabre, King and Pantling.

4. Stem angled; flowers about 2—2.5 mm. across; lateral sepals oblong, concave at the apex, deflexed; basal half of the narrow-triangular lip directed downwards, apical half directed forwards.

Lachen valley, 11,000′. VII.

H. gracile, King and Pantling.

— Stem terete; flowers 1—1.5 mm. across; lateral sepals falcate, not reflexed; lip with an expanded fleshy base having two deep oval pits, and a linear-oblong, nearly terete anterior part.

Singa-le-la, 12,000′; also Garhwal. VII.

H. pugioniforme, Lindley.

5. Leaves linear or linear-lanceolate, little or not at all narrowed towards the base of the blade, 10—20 times as long as broad; lip narrow-oblong or narrow-triangular, 2 to 4 times as long as broad; petals linear or linear-oblong 6

— Leaves obovate to oblanceolate, narrowed to the base of the blade, 3—8 times as long as broad; lip broad-ovate or trapezoidal, less than twice as long as broad; petals obliquely triangular 8

6. Leaves broad-linear or linear-lanceolate, 2; end-lobe of lip distinctly or much longer than the side-lobes; whole plant 10—30 cm. high 7

— Leaves narrow-linear, 2—3, 14—20 times as long as broad; whole plant 25—75 cm. high; spike narrow-cylindric, 7—25 cm. long; dorsal sepal and the linear petals connivent to form a hood, lateral sepals spreading; lip oblong, deflexed, with two minute auricles near the base, two filiform, curved side-lobes and a very short end-lobe.

4,500—9,500′, common; also from Garhwal to Tenasserim. VII, VIII.

H. angustifolium, Bentham.

7. Leaves linear-lanceolate, 15—18 cm. long; spike rather lax; sepals ovate-oblong; petals linear, acuminate; lip linear-oblong with a narrow triangular midlobe, two very small, but sometimes elongate, triangular

side-lobes and two very small triangular auricles above the base.

Tendong, 7,000′; Tankra, 9,500; Senchal and probably elsewhere. VIII.

H. quinquelobum, King and Pantling.

— Leaves broadly linear, 10—13 cm. long; spike dense; sepals broadly ovate to elliptic; petals narrow-oblong; lip triangular-oblong with two small, rounded basal lobes.

8—10,000′, common. VIII.

H. Jaffreyanum, King and Pantling,

8. Leaves inserted close to the base, obovate or oblanceolate, 3—10 cm. long; sepals nearly equal, the dorsal broad-ovate, the lateral oblong, somewhat spreading; lip trapezoidal, with very shallow, crenulate side-lobes and a triangular-ovate blunt end-lobe.

10—12,500′, common; also Nipal.

H. congestum, Lindley.

— Leaves inserted higher up, oblanceolate rather more than 10 cm. long; sepals unequal, dorsal broadly ovate to elliptic. lateral longer ovate-oblong, suberect; lip flat, broad-ovate, abruptly and shortly acuminate, edges shallowly crenulate. with a small basal pit and two low plates reaching the middle.

Lachen and Chumbi valleys, Cho-la and Pan-ka-la, 11—12,000′. VI, VII.

H. Josephi, Reichenbach fil.

DIPLOMERIS, Don.

1. Leaf solitary, sometimes with a much smaller one, inserted at the base of the very short stem, linear-oblong, 5—8 cm. long, 18—28 mm. broad, hairy; flowers solitary, 3—5 cm. long and 22—28 mm. across, white; sepals much smaller than the petals; petals reniform, lip shortly clawed, emarginate, with the thick midrib slightly projecting; spur funnel-shaped at the mouth, cylindric and curved towards the tip, considerably longer than the ovary.

   Tista valley, 1,000—1,400′, on the side of rocks; also Nipal and Bhotan. VI—VIII.

   D. hirsuta, Lindley.

SATYRIUM, Swartz.

1. Whole plant 50—75 cm. high; lower pair of leaves inserted 10—15 cm. above the ground, up to 25 cm. long and 9 cm. broad, elliptic-oblong; lower floral bracts about 2.5 cm. long, reflexed, lanceolate; petals entire; the two spurs rather variable in length and thickness, commonly twice as long as the ovary.

   8—10,000′; also in Bhotan, very common; from Kashmir to Upper Burma, and in Southern India. IX, X.

   S. nepalense, Don, *var.* **genuina.**

Whole plant less than 25 cm. high; lower pair of leaves inserted 2 4 cm. above the ground, 15 cm. and less long and 3 cm. broad, lanceolate-oblong; lower floral bracts less than 2 cm. long, reflexed, ovate, acuminate; sepals conspicuously ciliate; petals erose; spurs shorter than the sepals.

8—10,000′, Sikkim and Bhotan. IX, X.
S. nepalense, Don, *var.* **ciliata,** (Lindley).

CYPRIPEDIUM, Linnaeus.

1. Stemless; leaves 5—7, close to the ground, narrow-oblong to elliptic. 10—25 cm. long, 2.5—5 cm. broad, dark-green marbled with pale-green above and purple beneath; peduncle about twice as long as the leaves; flowers terminal, solitary, rarely two, 5—6.5 cm. across; dorsal sepal broadly ovate, white with green stripes; petals broad-linear, green and purplish with a few black spots; lip forming a cylindrical pouch, yellowish-green flushed with pink and reticulated green, inflexed lateral edges yellow.

   Tropical valleys, ascending to 4,000′. II, III. **C. venustum,** Wallich.

— With a stem; leaves inserted higher up, not marbled **2**

2. Leaves 2—3, close together, broadly ovate or nearly orbicular, 3—4 cm. long .. **3**

— Leaves 3—4, scattered, broadly elliptic to lanceolate, the largest 6—8 cm. long, and 2.5—5 cm. broad; flower brownish, about 6 cm. vertically and less than 5 cm., horizontally; dorsal sepal broad-ovate, lateral ovate-oblong, narrower, petals spreading, narrow-oblong; lip pendant, forming a broadly obovoid pouch having a wide crenate mouth, tinged purple.

Lachen and Chumbi valleys, 10—12,000′. VIII. **C. himalaicum,** Rolfe.

3. Height of flowering plant 12—30 cm.; leaves 3, alternate, broadly ovate or elliptic; peduncle slightly longer than the leaves; flower 5 cm. in diameter; lip longer than the sepals, brownish, flushed with bright purple near its crenulate mouth.

Lachen valley, 10,000′. VII.
C. tibeticum, King and Pantling.

— Height of flowering plant 10 cm. and less; leaves 2, opposite, nearly orbicular; peduncle shorter than the leaves; flower 2.5 cm. in diameter; lip shorter than the sepals, like sepals and petals brownish with darker brown lines.

Lachen valley, 10,000′. VII
C. elegans, Reichenbach fil.

APOSTASIA, Blume.

1. Stem rigid, up to 50 cm. high; leaves linear-lanceolate. 10—20 cm. long;

inflorescence a panicle consisting of spikes. 10—25 cm. long; flowers yellow, about 6 mm. across.

May yet be found in the Western parts of Sikkim; reported from Tropical Nipal, Khasia, Assam, the Malay Peninsula and Ceylon. **A. Wallichii,** R. Brown.

BULBOPHYLLUM, Thouars.

1. Pseudobulbs absent **2**

— Pseudobulbs present **6**

2. Leaves 12—32 mm. (½—1¼ in.) long flowers in clusters or small heads .. **3**

— Leaves 15—30 cm. (6—12 in.) long; flowers in racemes **4**

3. Rhizome thread-like; leaves ovate or elliptic, 25—30 mm. apart, not exceeding 18 mm. in length; the thread-like scape bearing 1—2 small flowers; sepals and petals yellowish with red streaks, lip purple.

   Lachung valley, 8,000′; also Khasia. V.

   B. hymenanthum, Hooker fil.

— Rhizome about 4 mm. thick; leaves oblong or oblanceolate, much narrowed near their base, 25—60 mm. long; the thread-like scape bearing a small head of flowers about 7—9 mm. in diameter; flowers dull-purple.

About 1,500′. IX, X.

B. gracilipes, King and Pantling.

4. Flowers in a dense, catkin-like, nodding raceme, black-purple; rhizome about 6 mm. thick.

6—7,000′; also Nipal, Assam, Khasia. X—I. **B. cylindraceum,** Lindley.

— Flowers in a somewhat lax, spike-like, erect or somewhat recurved raceme, yellowish-green or pale-green; rhizome 5 mm. and less thick 5

5. Rhizome clothed with brown fibres; spike rather abruptly bent away from the peduncle, rather sparsely flowered; flowers yellowish tinged with green and streaked with red; lip with purple spots.

5,000′. V, VI.

B. rigidum, King and Pantling.

— Rhizome nearly bare; spike straight, many-flowered; flowers pale-green.
Sivoke, 1,500′. VI.

B. ebulbum, King and Pantling.

6. Pseudobulbs crowded, either in clusters or in close-set rows 7

— Pseudobulbs distinctly, often widely separated from each other 16

7. Pseudobulbs globular, depressed-globular or depressed-top-shaped (turbinate) .. 8

— Pseudobulbs ovoid, ovoid-oblong or conical 11

8. Flowers in racemes 9

— Flowers in a small head; pseudobulbs globose, 9 mm. and less in diameter; leaf linear-lanceolate; head of flowers about 12 mm. across; sepals and petals pale reddish-brown with darker streaks, lip dark reddish-brown.

1,000′, rare. V.

B. piluliferum, King and Pantling.

9. Pseudobulbs globose; raceme erect or more or less bent sideways, not drooping .. 10

— Pseudobulbs depressed-turbinate with a large navel; raceme drooping, leafless at flowering time; flowers dull-purple, a line on the edge of the lip yellow.

Tista Valley, 1,500′, rare; also Tenasserim. III.

B. triste, Reichenbach fil.

10. Pseudobulbs 9—10 mm. in diameter; leaf narrow-oblong, 25—60 mm. long; sepals and petals pale-purple with darker nerves, petals with a darker blotch; lip dark-purple.

Chungtang and Tendong, 6—7,000′; also Naga Hills. VI, VII.

B. secundum, Hooker fil.

— Pseudobulbs 2—4 mm. in diameter; leaf obovate, 25—38 mm. long; sepals green, edged red-brown; petals green; lip yellow towards the outer edge.

Near base of Engo ridge, 2,500′. VII.

B. cornu-cervi, King and Pantling.

11. Pseudobulbs about 8—9 mm. long, each with a 25—30 mm. long leaf; flowers dull-lake-coloured..

British Bhotan, at Rumpti Lake, 1,000′. III. **B. Listeri,** King and Pantling.

— Pseudobulbs much larger **12**

12. Flowers in well-developed spikes or racemes, not spotted, 12 mm. and less in diameter **14**

— Flowers solitary, or two or three, arising from the base of the pseudobulbs, 18—26 mm. in diameter, spotted crimson or reddish-brown .. **13**

13. Pseudobulbs inverted pear-shaped, compressed, 25—38 mm. long; leaves elliptic-oblong, shortly petioled; blade 7—15 cm. long, 2.5—5 cm. broad; sepals and petals whitish or pale-ochraceous spotted with crimson; lip crimson or purple, spotted; the nectar having the smell of decaying fruit.

6,000, not uncommon; also Nipal and Khasia. X, XI. **B. leopardinum,** Wallich.

— Pseudobulbs ovoid, 15—20 mm. long; leaves broad-lanceolate, sessile, 3.5 to 5 cm. long, 1—1.3 cm. broad; flowers yellowish with reddish-brown spots.

Lachung, 9,000′; also Khasia. VIII.

B. Griffithii, Reichenbach fil.

14. Pseudobulbs ovoid or pear-shaped .. **15**

— Pseudobulbs slender-conical, nearly cylindric; scape 25 to nearly 50 cm. long, decurved; raceme 8—10 cm. long, rather lax; flowers green.

Sureil, 6,000′; Tonglu, 7,000′. VIII.

B. eublepharum, Reichenbach fil.

15. Spike pendulous on an erect scape; leaves flaccid, broadly lanceolate or oblanceolate, sessile; sepals pale yellow-green outside, white inside; petals green; lip yellow with a papillose margin.

3—6,000′, common; also Nipal to Burma. X—I. **B. hirtum,** Lindley.

— Spike bent aside or decurved, but not pendulous, on a flexuous scape; leaves narrowed into a channelled petiole; flowers brown; lip conspicuously fringed.

Bhotan, 6,000′; also Burma. VIII, IX.

B. penicillium, Parish and Reichenbach fil.

16. Pseudobulbs at flowering time depressed-turbinate or cake-shaped, broader than high **17**

— Pseudobulbs globular or more frequently ovoid, ovoid-oblong or ovoid-subcylindric, either as high as broad or higher than broad **18**

17. Pseudobulbs no more than 1 cm. apart, (often crowded), at flowering time with a conspicuous navel and leafless; raceme drooping on an erect scape and about half as long as the latter, about 3—6 cm. long; flowers dull-purple, lip lined yellow along the edge.
Tista Valley, 1,500′. III.
B. triste, Reichenbach fil.

Pseudobulbs about 6 to 7 cm. apart, one-leaved: scape and raceme erect, both together 20 to 25 cm. long; flowers yellowish-white.
Tropical Valleys, up to 4,000′. IX.
B. Thomsoni, Hooker fil.

18. Rhizome about 1—2.5 mm. thick, often thread-like **19**

— Rhizome about 4—5 mm. thick .. **27**

19. Inflorescence erect or directed obliquely upwards **20**

— Inflorescence pendent, ovoid-oblong in outline; flowers 12—15, crowded, purplish, scape thread-like; spurs parallel to dorsal sepal and to petals; sepals dull purple with edges and keels green; petals pale purple with dark-purple tips; lip purple with yellow tip; pseudobulbs ovoid, about 2 cm. long.

Nangbi, 5—6,000′; also Khasia. IX.

B. bisetum, Lindley.

20. Flowers in umbels, loose clusters or lax racemes **21**

— Flowers forming a compact head, white except the yellow-tinged sepals, sweet-smelling; pseudobulbs subcylindric, 18—25 mm. long; leaf linear-oblong or lanceolate, 2.5—8 cm. long; lip fleshy, the central groove and the edges beset with capitate hairs.

3—7,000′, common; also Nipal to Tenasserim. V—IX. **B. odoratissimum,** Lindley.

21. Flowers 2—6 in small umbels **22**

— Flowers 4—8 forming lax racemes .. **26**

22. Sepals and petals with purple stripes on a yellowish-green ground; leaves with a channelled stalk and an elliptic 2.5—6.5 cm. long blade marked on either half with about 5 fine nerves; pseudobulbs broad-ovoid; scape 5—8 cm. long, bearing 2—4 spreading flowers.

Senchal, 7,000′; also Khasia. IX.

B. striatum, Reichenbach fil.

— Sepals and petals not striped; leaves sessile **23**

23. Pseudobulbs 4—5 mm. thick, cylindric or narrowly inverted pear-shaped; lip lanceolate 24

— Pseudobulbs 8—10 mm. thick, broadly ellipsoidal to ellipsoidal or ovoid-oblong; lip ovate-oblong 25

24. Pseudobulbs cylindric; rhizome about 2 mm. thick; distance between the pseudobulbs 2.5—3.0 cm.; leaf-blades nearly straight, narrow-oblong; flowers pale-yellow except the orange upper part of the sepals and the concave part of the lip.

Tropical Valleys, 1,500 to 2,000′; also Tenasserim. VII.

B. protractum, Hooker fil.

— Pseudobulbs slender inverted-pear-shaped or nearly stout-cylindric, always thicker near the base; rhizome about 1 mm. thick; distance between pseudobulbs about 4 to 10 cm.; leaf-blades recurved, lanceolate; flowers pale-yellowish-green.

On Engo. 5—7,000′; forms tangled masses. VII, VIII **B. Gamblei,** Hooker fil.

25. Rhizome about 1 mm. thick; pseudobulbs ellipsoid to ellipsoid-oblong, 10—15 mm. long; leaf 25—32 mm. long, elliptic-oblong to lanceolate; sepals and petals white tinged orange red at their tip; lip yellow or yellowish-white.

Western Bhotan Duars; Kumai forest. 1,500′. VI.

B. Clarkeanum, King and Pantling.

— Rhizome about 2 mm. thick; pseudobulbs ovoid-oblong to nearly cylindric, 25—30 mm. long; leaf 5.5—70 mm. long, broad-linear; flowers pale-yellowish-green, a blotch near the foot of the column orange, Mangpu, 3,000′; also Khasia. VII.

B. leptanthum, Hooker fil.

26. Distance between pseudobulbs 3 cm. and less; leaf broadly linear, about 6 cm. long, deciduous; pseudobulbs globular or shortly ovoid, 6—12 mm. long; scape filiform, about 10 cm. long; raceme one-sided, inclined, consisting of about six pale-yellowish flowers.

Tista Valley, 1,500′. IV.

B. polyrrhizum, Lindley.

— Distance between pseudobulbs 6 cm. and more; leaf lanceolate-linear, 8—15 cm. long; pseudobulbs inverted-pear-shaped, about 2 cm. long; scapes shorter or longer than the leaves; raceme all-sided; flowers yellowish or buff, purple-spotted.

5,000—7,000′, common; also Nipal to Khasia. X—XII. **B. reptans,** Lindley.

27. Pseudobulbs ovoid-oblong to ovoid-cylindrical, 36—100 mm. long . . . . . . **28.**

— Pseudobulbs broadly ovoid, 22—45 mm. long . . . . **29.**

28. Rhizome simple, densely rooting all along; pseudobulbs about 5 cm. apart; leaves

linear-oblong, 7—18 cm. long; flowers solitary, rising singly or in pairs from the base of, or between the pseudobulbs, 18—24 mm. long, pale-green with purple nerves; lip edged dark-purple.

Tista Valley, 2,000′; also Nipal and Khasia. VI, VII. **B. affine,** Lindley.

— Rhizome branched, rooting at the nodes; pseudobulbs 7—8 cm. apart; leaves ovate-oblong, 5—10 cm. long; flowers in small clusters of 4—5, 12—15 mm. long, green flushed with brown, tips of sepals yellow.

Sittong, 5—6,000′; also Khasia. VII.

B. cauliflorum, Hooker fil.

29. Pseudobulbs 15—18 cm. apart, smooth, about 3 cm. long; leaves oblong-linear, 12—22 cm. long, about 3 cm. broad; flowers in a lax erect (without the peduncle), 12—15 cm. long raceme, white and yellow.

Engo, 3,000′, Rishap; also Bhotan and Khasia. XI, XII.

B. gymnopus, Hooker fil.

— Pseudobulbs 7—10 cm. apart, ribbed, about 4 cm. long; leaves broad-lanceolate, 12—25 cm. long, about 4—4.5 cm. broad; flowers in a dense, catkin-like, 5—8 cm. long, decurved spike, copper-brown, of a disagreeable odour.

Warm valleys, common; also from Nipal to Burma. X—XII.

B. Careyanum, Sprengel.

IONE, Lindley.

1. Scape 1—2-flowered **2**

— Scape ending in a 5—10-flowered raceme .. **3**

2. Flowers about 9 mm. across; sepals and petals yellowish, lip purple.
Bhotan, Buxa, 6,000′. IV.

I. Andersoni, King and Pantling.

— Flowers about 12 mm. across, pale-green. Tendong, 6,000′.

I. intermedia, King and Pantling.

3. Pseudobulbs 12—18 mm. long; leaves 6—10 cm. long, 6—10 mm. broad; flower-bearing scape shorter than the leaf; flowers in two rows, about 10 mm. long; sepals and petals pale and translucent with claret-coloured nerves; lip claret-coloured, with the outer part of the margins serrate and the upper surface with a projecting swelling.
6,000—7,000′, very common; also Nipal, Bhotan and Khasia. X—XI.

I. bicolor, Lindley.

— Pseudobulbs 30—36 mm. long; leaves 10—20 cm. long and 18—28 mm. broad; flower bearing scape much longer than the leaf; flowers arranged in one row, 22—28 mm. long, drooping; sepals and petals translucent, greenish-white, with a network of pink veins; lip dark-purple, upper surface with a two-chambered swelling, edges entire or crenulate.

About 6,000′; also in Bhotan; very common. X, XI.

(*This is the same species as that incorrectly named I. brevipes, see page* 102.)

I. paleacea, Lindley.

SUNIPIA, Lindley.

Pseudobulbs ovoid, spongy, 18—30 mm. long, on a stout rhizome; leaf broadly lanceolate, 10—15 cm. long, 18—25 mm. broad; peduncle slender, raceme deflexed; flowers in two rows, numerous, supported by conspicuous, boat-shaped bracts; sepals unequal, the lateral ones longer, like the petals and lip greenish, flushed with purple.

3,000—4,000′; also Nipal to Tenasserim. IV, V.

(*This is the same species as Ione scariosa, see page* 102.)

Sunipia scariosa, Lindley.